FOR ME, THE FIRST
YEARS ARE LOST.

NOW, IN A PLACE AS CROWDED AS THIS, I'M AFRAID WE'LL NEVER BE FOUND.

I DON'T SEE HER, HASSAN.
HOOYO.

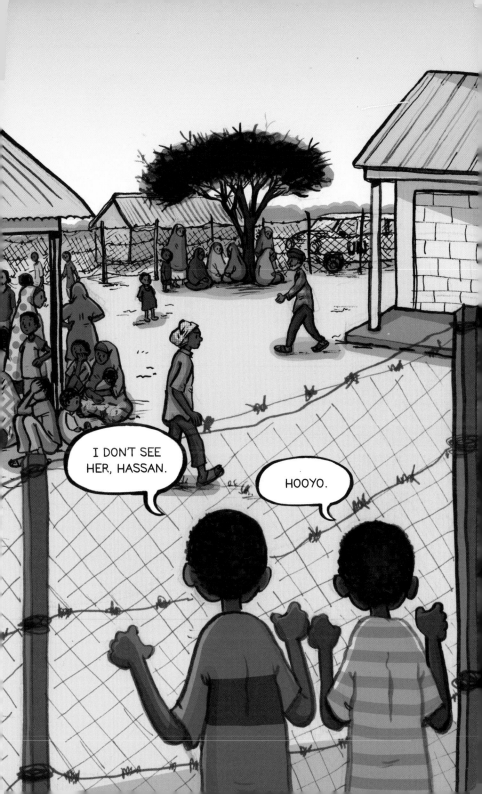

C'MON, IT'S GETTING LATE. WE SHOULD GO BACK HOME.
WE STAY OFF THE MAIN ROADS TO TRY AND AVOID TROUBLE.
UNHCR
HURRY, HASSAN.
RIGHT NOW, WE'RE RIGHT SMACK DAB IN THE MIDDLE OF **A3** BLOCK, AND HASSAN AND I LIVE IN BLOCK **A2**. LET'S JUST SAY IT'S NOT A GOOD IDEA TO BE CAUGHT IN ANOTHER BLOCK ALL ALONE. THAT'S HOW A GROUP OF KIDS STOLE OUR SHOES AND TROUSERS LAST WEEK.

AS SOON AS WE GET BACK TO A2, I BREATHE A SIGH OF RELIEF. IN OUR BLOCK, EVERYONE KNOWS ME AND MY BROTHER. NO ONE WILL BOTHER US.

WALKING WITH HASSAN SOMETIMES TAKES A WHILE. HE STOPS TO GREET EVERY NEIGHBOUR WE MEET.

IF HE SEES SOMEONE PUSHING A WHEELBARROW, HE LIKES TO HELP OUT.

HE SAYS HELLO TO THE DONKEYS PULLING CARTS.

HE COLLECTS FRUIT TO HAND OUT TO ALL THE NEIGHBOURHOOD GOATS.

BY THE TIME WE GET HOME, IT'S NEARLY NIGHTTIME. FATUMA DOESN'T LIKE US TO WALK AROUND WHEN IT'S DARK.

HASSAN AND I LIVE HERE.

FATUMA LIVES RIGHT ACROSS THE PATH. SHE'S KIND OF LIKE OUR FOSTER MUM. SHE WATCHES OVER US TO MAKE SURE WE'RE OK.

ALHAMDULILLAH! **THERE** YOU ARE! I WAS STARTING TO GET WORRIED!

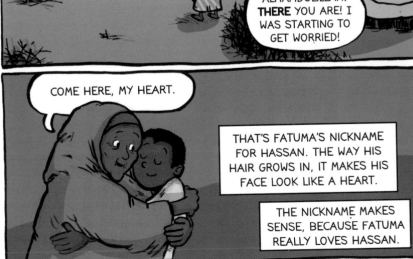

COME HERE, MY HEART.

THAT'S FATUMA'S NICKNAME FOR HASSAN. THE WAY HIS HAIR GROWS IN, IT MAKES HIS FACE LOOK LIKE A HEART.

THE NICKNAME MAKES SENSE, BECAUSE FATUMA REALLY LOVES HASSAN.

YOU TOO, OMAR! MY BIG BOY!
OK, SHE REALLY LOVES **BOTH** OF US.
WE DON'T HAVE ANY FOOD TO EAT TONIGHT, SO HASSAN AND I GO RIGHT TO BED.
HASSAN AND I SLEEP IN OUR OWN TENT. AFTER ALL, FATUMA IS NOT OUR **REAL** MUM, SO WE'RE STILL ASSIGNED DIFFERENT TENTS.
UNROLL
HASSAN DOESN'T SLEEP VERY WELL, AND I DON'T EITHER. I USUALLY TELL STORIES ABOUT OUR HOME IN SOMALIA TO HELP US BOTH FALL ASLEEP.

BUT I STILL WAKE UP WITH NIGHTMARES.
DAD!
JUDGING BY THE SOUNDS ALL AROUND US, I'M NOT THE ONLY ONE WITH BAD DREAMS.
MUNIRA!
AMAN!
NO!
STOP!

CHAPTER 1

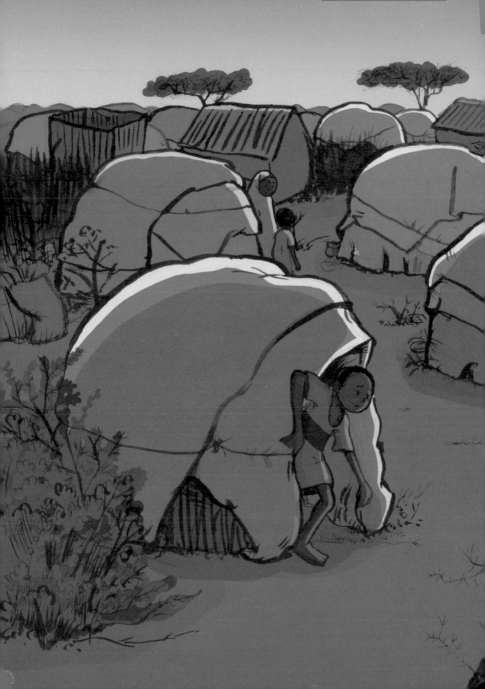

MY BROTHER AND I LIVE HERE: IN A REFUGEE CAMP IN KENYA, IN AFRICA. THE CAMP IS CALLED DADAAB.

WE WEREN'T BORN HERE. HASSAN AND I WERE BORN IN SOMALIA. SOME PEOPLE HERE ARE FROM ETHIOPIA OR SUDAN OR OTHER PLACES IN AFRICA. BUT WE ALL HAVE ONE THING IN COMMON: WE HAD TO LEAVE OUR HOMES BECAUSE WE WERE AFRAID FOR OUR LIVES.

SOME PEOPLE WHO LIVE HERE HOPE THEY'LL BE SENT TO AMERICA OR CANADA OR SOME OTHER PLACE TO LIVE. NOT ME, THOUGH. I JUST WANT THE WAR IN SOMALIA TO END SO WE CAN GO BACK HOME. OUR MUM WILL BE ABLE TO FIND US THERE.

DADAAB IS SO BIG, IT'S ACTUALLY MADE UP OF THREE SEPARATE CAMPS. YOU CAN TAKE A BUS FROM ONE CAMP TO ANOTHER...OR YOU CAN WALK FOR ABOUT FOUR HOURS. THERE'S **HAGADERA**, WHICH IS NAMED AFTER THE BIG TREES. THERE'S **DAGAHALEY**, NAMED AFTER...I DON'T KNOW WHAT.
I LIVE IN **IFO** CAMP, WHICH IN ENGLISH ROUGHLY TRANSLATES TO "CITY OF LIGHT".
DON'T LET THE NAME FOOL YOU, THOUGH—WE DON'T HAVE ELECTRICITY HERE.
AFTER SO MANY YEARS, WITH SO MANY PEOPLE LIVING HERE, IFO IS MORE LIKE A CITY THAN A CAMP. WE HAVE MARKETS, SCHOOLS, MOSQUES, A HOSPITAL...EVERYTHING.

REFUGEE CAMPS ARE SUPPOSED TO BE A TEMPORARY PLACE TO STAY UNTIL IT'S SAFE TO GO BACK HOME. I GUESS NO ONE EXPECTED THE WAR TO LAST SO LONG, THOUGH, BECAUSE HASSAN AND I HAVE BEEN HERE FOR SEVEN YEARS.

THERE ARE A LOT OF BAD PARTS ABOUT LIVING IN A REFUGEE CAMP. THERE'S NOT A LOT OF FOOD HERE, SO HASSAN AND I ARE ALWAYS HUNGRY. AND IT'S **HOT**. BUT FOR ME, ONE OF THE WORST PARTS OF LIVING IN A REFUGEE CAMP IS...IT'S **REALLY BORING**. EVERY DAY IS BASICALLY THE SAME!

THE FIRST THING I DO EVERY DAY, AFTER MORNING PRAYERS, IS I FETCH WATER. THAT CAN TAKE **HOURS**. THERE'S ONLY ONE WATER SPIGOT AND IT'S ONLY OPEN A FEW HOURS A DAY—SO THERE'S ALWAYS A REALLY LONG LINE.

AFTER THAT, I CLEAN OUR TENT AND MAKE SURE ANYTHING VALUABLE IS HIDDEN AWAY.

THEN HASSAN AND I GO TO FATUMA'S TENT. SHE MAKES US TEA. IF THERE'S ANYTHING TO EAT, WE EAT.

I ASKED AROUND AND I FOUND ANOTHER PAIR OF SHORTS FOR YOU AND HASSAN. I'M AFRAID YOU'LL HAVE TO WAIT FOR SHOES.

WOW, THANKS, FATUMA!

TRUTH BE TOLD, HASSAN WOULD RATHER BE SHORTS-LESS.

PUT. THEM. ON!

NNNN!

HI, OMAR!

OH, HEY, JERI.

THAT'S MY BEST FRIEND, JERI. I'VE KNOWN HIM PRACTICALLY MY WHOLE LIFE.

FOOTBALL AFTER SCHOOL, RIGHT?

YEAH, FOR SURE!

JERI USED TO STAY HOME LIKE ME, BECAUSE HE WAS SICK. THAT'S HOW HE GOT HIS NICKNAME: "JERI" IS A NAME FOR SOMEONE WHO LIMPS. BUT NOW HE GOES TO SCHOOL WITH A LOT OF OTHER KIDS FROM OUR BLOCK.

I'VE NEVER GONE TO SCHOOL. I'VE ALWAYS STAYED HOME TO TAKE CARE OF HASSAN. I'M THE OLDEST, SO IT'S MY JOB TO PROTECT HIM.

BUT I WONDER WHAT SCHOOL WOULD BE LIKE.

C'MON, LET'S GO TO THE BUILDING PIT.

"BUILDING PIT" IS A NICE WAY TO DESCRIBE THIS PLACE. IT'S REALLY JUST A PUDDLE WHERE WE PLAY IN THE MUD. YOU HAVE TO BE CREATIVE IN A REFUGEE CAMP.

YOU MAKE THE BRICKS, HASSAN, AND I'LL BUILD THE HOUSE.

ONE...TWO...

EVEN THOUGH I'VE NEVER GONE TO AN ACTUAL SCHOOL, MY MUM TAUGHT ME ALL MY NUMBERS WHEN I WAS SMALL. I KEEP PRACTISING SO I WON'T FORGET.

2 BRICKS PLUS 2 BRICKS EQUALS...4 BRICKS!

HE CAN'T SAY SO, BUT I CAN TELL HASSAN IS IMPRESSED BY MY AMAZING MATHS SKILLS.

HASSAN CAN'T TALK. EVER SINCE HE WAS A BABY, HE'S ONLY EVER SAID ONE WORD.

HOOYO!

BUT HE MAKES A LOT OF NOISES, AND WE UNDERSTAND EACH OTHER.

THE DOCTORS SAY HASSAN IS DOING BETTER NOW. HE USED TO HAVE A LOT OF SEIZURES WHEN HE WAS YOUNGER. THOSE WERE REALLY SCARY. BUT HE HASN'T HAD ONE IN A WHILE.

I DON'T LIKE TO THINK ABOUT THOSE SEIZURES. I DON'T KNOW WHAT I WOULD DO WITHOUT MY BROTHER. HE MAKES LIFE HERE BEARABLE.

HASSAN AND I ALWAYS PLAY THE SAME GAME AT THE BUILDING PIT: **HOUSE**. IT TAKES ALMOST ALL DAY TO DO IT PROPERLY. BUT FINALLY...

FINISHED! NOW, THIS IS OUR HOUSE. IT'S BIG ENOUGH FOR YOU, ME, FATUMA AND MAMA.

OVER THERE ARE OUR CORNFIELDS.

AND WAY OVER THERE IS WHERE WE KEEP THE GOATS! WE HAVE 100...NO, **200** GOATS!

AND THAT IS THE SCHOOL. IN THE AFTERNOON I'LL GO TO SCHOOL, AND YOU'LL GO HOME AND HELP MAMA WITH THE GOATS.

LOOK, WE HAVE A NICE, SOFT MATTRESS TO SLEEP ON. IT FEELS LIKE A CLOUD!

YOU GOT ROOM ON THAT MATTRESS FOR ME?

SCOOT OVER.

IF ANY OF THE OTHER BOYS CAUGHT ME PLAYING HOUSE, I'D BE EMBARRASSED—BUT I'M NEVER EMBARRASSED AROUND JERI.

ALL OF A SUDDEN, THE GROUND STARTS TO SHAKE AND THE DUST KICKS UP. THIS CAN ONLY MEAN ONE THING...

...THE OTHER **A2** BOYS ARE HOME FROM SCHOOL TOO.

C'MON, IT'S FOOTBALL TIME!

THERE ARE A LOT OF KIDS LIVING HERE IN A2. LIKE JERI, A LOT OF THEM GO BY NICKNAMES, SINCE MANY SOMALI NAMES ARE SIMILAR. THAT'S **TALL** ALI, FOR EXAMPLE, AND HE'S **SHORT** ALI.

I HAVE A NICKNAME TOO...

HEY, **DANTEY**! YOU GONNA PLAY WITH **US**, OR LIMPY HERE?

"DANTEY" MEANS...SOMEONE WHO KIND OF KEEPS TO THEMSELVES. IT WAS MY DAD'S NICKNAME TOO, BACK IN SOMALIA. ONE OF MY NEIGHBOURS TOLD ME THAT. SO I GUESS HE WAS KIND OF QUIET LIKE ME. SO I DON'T MIND IF KIDS PICK ON ME FOR BEING QUIET, IF IT MEANS I AM LIKE MY DAD.

LIMP OR NO LIMP, JERI CAN RUN CIRCLES AROUND **YOU**, TALL ALI. I'M ON HIS TEAM.

TALL ALI IS KIND OF A JERK, BUT THE A2 KIDS STICK TOGETHER ANYWAY. WE PLAY FOOTBALL EVERY DAY. ONE PROBLEM: WE DON'T HAVE A FOOTBALL BALL, SO WE HAVE TO **MAKE** ONE OUT OF PLASTIC BAGS.

THE ONLY PROBLEM WITH **THAT** IS...

KICK

...THEY DON'T LAST VERY LONG.

AW, MAN.

MOVE IT, YOU IDIOT!

OW!

LOOK, I HAVE ONE, TWO, THREE!

HEY, JERI, WHAT'S HE TALKING ABOUT? "WON TOO TREE"?

NO! IT'S "ONE, TWO, THREE"! IT'S HOW YOU COUNT TO THREE IN ENGLISH. WE LEARNED IT IN SCHOOL TODAY.

ONE, TWO... TREE?

NO, THHHHH-REEEE! YOU HAVE TO STICK YOUR TONGUE OUT, LIKE THIS. THHH-REEE. THHHHH-REEEE.

ONE...TWO...THHHHHREE. ONE... TWO...THHHHREEEE.

IF I LISTENED CAREFULLY WHILE THE BOYS TALKED, IT WAS **ALMOST** LIKE I GOT TO GO TO SCHOOL.

HEY... HASSAN? **HASSAN!** WHERE ARE YOU?

I DON'T LIKE TO LOSE SIGHT OF HASSAN. HE'D BE FINE IN OUR BLOCK, OF COURSE, BUT IF HE WANDERS INTO A3 OR A4...

I SEE HIM, OVER THERE. WITH TALL ALI.

HASSAN! I TOLD YOU NOT TO RUN AWAY!

...WHAT ARE YOU DOING?

WATCH THIS! HASSAN, BOO-HOO-HOO!

BOO-HOO!

WHENEVER HASSAN SEES SOMEONE CRYING, HE STARTS TO CRY TOO. HE CAN'T HELP IT.

KNOCK IT OFF!

WHAT? IT'S FUNNY! BOO-HOO-HOO!

HASSAN, IT'S OK. IT'S NOT SAD. WE'RE **HAPPY**, OK? **HAPPY**.

JERI WALKED HOME WITH ME AND HASSAN, LIKE HE'S DONE HUNDREDS OF TIMES BEFORE.

FORGET ABOUT TALL ALI, HASSAN. HE MAKES FUN OF ME ALL THE TIME, AND LOOK HOW BADLY WE BEAT HIM AT FOOTBALL. DON'T LET HIM GET TO YOU.

C'MON, HASSAN. LET'S PRACTICE YOUR ENGLISH. SAY, "ONE, TWO, THREE"!

HOOYO!

UMM...NO.

LISTEN, HASSAN, YOU'RE GOING TO HAVE TO LEARN ENGLISH IF YOU WANT TO LIVE IN AMERICA!

HOW MANY TIMES HAVE I TOLD YOU?! WE'RE NOT GOING TO AMERICA. WE'RE GOING BACK TO SOMALIA WHEN THE WAR'S OVER.

YOU'RE CRAZY. MY DAD'S FRIEND'S COUSIN JUST GOT SENT TO AMERICA, AND HE SENDS BACK MONEY EVERY MONTH. EVERYONE THERE IS SUPER RICH!

MY DAD SAYS IN AMERICA, EVERYONE HAS BIG CARS AND BIG HOUSES. MY DAD ALMOST HAS ALL OF OUR PAPERWORK READY FOR THE UN.*

WELL, **WE'RE** GOING BACK TO SOMALIA TO TAKE CARE OF OUR HOUSE AND OUR FARM.

"AND TO FIND MY MUMMY." I DIDN'T ADD THAT LAST PART— I DIDN'T WANT JERI TO THINK I'M A **COMPLETE** BABY.

HASSAN, BACK ME UP HERE! WHICH WOULD YOU RATHER HAVE: A BIG CAR, OR A FARM?!

HOOYO!

I'M PRETTY SURE HE SAID "CAR."

YEAH, RIGHT!

JERI! MY OTHER SON! COME HAVE TEA WITH US.

THANK YOU, FATUMA, BUT I HAVE TO GET HOME. SEE YOU LATER, OMAR! BYE, HASSAN.

I HAVE A SPECIAL TREAT FOR YOU BOYS TODAY— SUGAR FOR YOUR TEA!

MMM!

*UN STANDS FOR THE UNITED NATIONS. UNHCR, OR THE UNITED NATIONS HIGH COMMISSIONER FOR REFUGEES, IS AN AGENCY THAT HELPS REFUGEES AROUND THE WORLD.

FATUMA, GUESS WHAT I LEARNED HOW TO SAY. "ONE, TWO, THREE." THAT'S HOW YOU COUNT IN ENGLISH!

OH, MY!

AND LOOK, JERI TAUGHT ME HOW TO WRITE MY NAME IN ENGLISH TOO.

Hello my name is Omar

LIFE IN THE CAMP WAS NOT EASY...BUT HASSAN AND I WERE TOGETHER. WE HAD FATUMA. I WAS LEARNING NEW THINGS. AND AS SOON AS THE WAR ENDED IN SOMALIA, WE COULD GO BACK HOME.

BACK HOME, WE'D BE SAFE. NO ONE WOULD BOTHER HASSAN, AND WE WOULD FIND MY MOTHER.

WE'D BEEN WAITING FOR **SEVEN LONG YEARS** TO GO HOME. HOW MUCH LONGER COULD IT BE?

CHAPTER 2

EVERY DAY IN A REFUGEE CAMP IS THE SAME...

EXCEPT WHEN IT'S **NOT**. SOMETIMES YOUR LIFE CAN CHANGE IN AN INSTANT, BUT YOU CAN NEVER BE SURE IF IT'S A **GOOD** CHANGE OR A **BAD** CHANGE.

<HELLO, OMAR. MY NAME IS SALAN.>*

<HELLO, SALAN. IT IS NICE TO MEET YOU.>

I'D SEEN THIS GUY AROUND BEFORE—I'M PRETTY SURE HE LIVED IN MY BLOCK. ALL THE KIDS CALL HIM TALL SALAN, BECAUSE, WELL...YOU CAN GUESS WHY.

YOU SPEAK ENGLISH VERY WELL! AND YOU CAN WRITE IT TOO! YOU MUST DO VERY WELL IN SCHOOL.

UMM...

* < > DENOTES ENGLISH

UNTIL I'M SURE THAT SOMEONE IS SAFE, I TRY TO KEEP HASSAN AWAY FROM NEW PEOPLE.

SALAN SEEMED ALL RIGHT, THOUGH.

<HELLO. MY NAME IS SALAN. WHAT IS YOUR NAME?>

HE DOESN'T TALK.

YOU DON'T SPEAK ENGLISH LIKE OMAR HERE?

NO, HE DOESN'T TALK. AT ALL.
... WELL, EXCEPT HE SAYS "HOOYO" A LOT.

OH. AND WHERE ARE YOUR PARENTS?

OUR FATHER DIED IN SOMALIA. BUT OUR MOTHER IS ALIVE. SOMEWHERE. WE JUST DON'T KNOW WHERE.

SO IT'S JUST YOU AND YOUR BROTHER HERE?

AND FATUMA. SHE'S OUR FOSTER MUM.

I SEE. OMAR, I'M HERE TODAY TO INTRODUCE MYSELF. I AM A COMMUNITY LEADER, SO IF YOU HAVE ANY PROBLEMS AT ALL—WITH YOUR FOOD RATIONS, YOUR NEIGHBOURS, OR SCHOOL—YOU CAN COME TO ME, AND WE'LL TRY TO SORT IT OUT.

SPEAKING OF SCHOOL...IT'S THE MIDDLE OF THE DAY. WHY AREN'T YOU IN CLASS RIGHT NOW?

I...I DON'T GO TO SCHOOL.

OH? AND WHY IS THAT?

I DON'T NEED TO GO TO SCHOOL TO LEARN HOW TO TAKE CARE OF MY BROTHER, DO I?

SALAN GOT A KIND OF THOUGHTFUL LOOK ON HIS FACE AS HE WALKED AWAY.

NO.

NO, I DON'T SUPPOSE YOU DO. I'LL SEE YOU LATER, HASSAN. <GOODBYE, OMAR.>

I STARTED SEEING TALL SALAN PRETTY OFTEN AFTER THAT. HE WAS ALWAYS VISITING WITH NEIGHBOURS, GETTING TO KNOW THEM AND LISTENING TO THEIR COMPLAINTS. I LIKED TO PRACTICE NEW ENGLISH PHRASES WITH HIM.

<LOVELY WEATHER TODAY!>

<EXCUSE ME, DO YOU HAVE THE TIME?>

<WOULD YOU LIKE A CUP OF TEA?>

ONE DAY I FOUND HIM TALKING WITH FATUMA.

OMAR, WE WERE JUST TALKING ABOUT YOU. COME, HAVE A SEAT.

FATUMA LOOKED WORRIED.

IS EVERYTHING OK, FATUMA?

SALAN WAS JUST TELLING ME HIS THOUGHTS ABOUT YOU.

I DIDN'T DO IT!

NO, NO. YOU DIDN'T DO ANYTHING WRONG.

SALAN THINKS YOU SHOULD GO TO SCHOOL.

AND **I** TOLD HIM WE HAVE BIGGER PROBLEMS IN OUR LIFE THAN SCHOOL. WHY BOTHER WITH SCHOOL WHEN WE BARELY HAVE ENOUGH TO EAT?

THE WORLD IS CHANGING, FATUMA. WHO KNOWS WHERE ANY OF US WILL END UP IN THE NEXT FEW YEARS? WITH AN EDUCATION, HE'LL BE PREPARED FOR WHATEVER COMES NEXT.

WHAT DO **YOU** THINK, OMAR? DO YOU WANT TO GO TO SCHOOL, OR NOT?

I...BUT I **CAN'T** GO TO SCHOOL. WHO WILL TAKE CARE OF HASSAN?

FATUMA IS HIS LEGAL GUARDIAN, NO? SHE'LL WATCH OVER HIM WHILE YOU'RE GONE. IT'S ONLY A FEW HOURS EVERY DAY.

BUT...WE'RE NEVER APART! I'M HIS BIG BROTHER. HE...HE NEEDS ME!

FATUMA TELLS ME THAT HASSAN HAS LOTS OF FRIENDS AROUND THE NEIGHBOURHOOD.

DOES HE NEED YOU EVERY **HOUR** OF EVERY **DAY**? DOESN'T HASSAN NEED TO LEARN SOME INDEPENDENCE TOO?

I THOUGHT ABOUT THIS. EVERYONE IN A2 KNOWS HASSAN. MAYBE HE WOULD BE FINE WITH FATUMA.

...THEN AGAIN, I KNEW WHAT COULD HAPPEN TO FAMILIES WHEN THEY LEFT ONE ANOTHER.

WELL THEN...WHAT ABOUT HIS SEIZURES? DID FATUMA TELL YOU ABOUT **THEM**?

SHE DID. SHE ALSO SAID IT'S BEEN OVER A YEAR SINCE HE'S HAD ONE, AND SHE KNOWS HOW TO HANDLE THEM.

OK, WELL, WHAT DO I NEED TO GO TO SCHOOL FOR, ANYWAY? SOON WE'LL BE BACK IN SOMALIA AND I'LL BE A FARMER LIKE MY DAD!

FARMERS NEED TO KNOW HOW TO READ AND COUNT! BESIDES, THE CIVIL WAR HAS BEEN RAGING FOR YEARS NOW, AND FIGHTING IS GETTING WORSE. NEW REFUGEES ARRIVE HERE EVERY WEEK. I'M SORRY, BUT RIGHT NOW THERE IS NO SOMALIA TO RETURN TO.

SO? WHAT'S YOUR PLAN B?

MAYBE WE'LL BE SENT TO AMERICA!

OH? AND HOW MANY PEOPLE DO YOU KNOW WHO HAVE BEEN RESETTLED TO AMERICA?

WELL...NONE. BUT JERI'S DAD'S FRIEND'S COUSIN...

COME WITH ME.

OMAR. LOOK AT THIS GRAIN OF SAND. THIS IS YOU.

FLING

YOU ARE ONE OF THOUSANDS—OF **HUNDREDS** OF THOUSANDS OF REFUGEES HERE IN DADAAB. YOU'RE ABOUT AS LIKELY TO GET CHOSEN TO GO TO AMERICA AS I AM TO FIND THAT GRAIN OF SAND AGAIN.

BUT WE **MIGHT** GET CHOSEN...

YES. OR YOU MIGHT **NOT** GET CHOSEN. YOU AND HASSAN COULD SPEND YOUR ENTIRE LIVES IN THIS REFUGEE CAMP. THEN WHAT?

SPEND MY WHOLE **LIFE** HERE? THAT THOUGHT WAS...DEPRESSING.

OMAR, ONLY GOD KNOWS WHAT WILL HAPPEN IN THE FUTURE. BUT IF YOU GET AN EDUCATION, YOU'LL BE PREPARED. YOU COULD GET A JOB. YOU COULD START A SCHOOL, LIKE I DID. YOU COULD PROVIDE FOR YOURSELF AND YOUR FAMILY.

YOU HAVE A GIFT, OMAR. YOU'RE SMART. AND WHEN GOD GIVES YOU A GIFT, IT IS YOUR JOB TO USE IT.

BUT...BUT I CAN'T. I CAN'T GO TO SCHOOL! I JUST **CAN'T**!

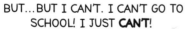

33

I...I'VE NEVER GONE TO SCHOOL BEFORE. IF I START NOW, THEY'LL PUT ME IN A CLASS WITH THE BABIES.

KICK

HA HA HA HA HA HA HA HA HA HA HA HA HA HA

IT WASN'T FUNNY. I DIDN'T SEE WHY HE WAS LAUGHING.

OMAR. YOU LIVE IN A REFUGEE CAMP. YOU BARELY HAVE ENOUGH FOOD TO SURVIVE... AND YOU'RE WORRIED ABOUT BEING IN THE SAME CLASS WITH SEVEN-YEAR-OLDS?! HA-HA-HA!

HA HA HA HA

TELL YOU WHAT. I KNOW THE HEAD TEACHER OF THE PRIMARY SCHOOL. HOW ABOUT I ASK HIM IF YOU CAN BE PLACED IN YEAR SIX WITH KIDS YOUR OWN AGE? THEN WE CAN ALL TALK AGAIN.

I GUESS SO.

WHY WAS HE STILL LAUGHING? THIS GUY NEEDED TO GET OUT MORE.

FATUMA STILL LOOKED WORRIED WHEN TALL SALAN LEFT. HASSAN LOOKED WORRIED TOO.

AND ME?

...I DIDN'T KNOW HOW TO FEEL.

DAYS PASSED, AND I DIDN'T SEE TALL SALAN. HE DIDN'T COME, AND HE DIDN'T COME, AND HE DIDN'T COME.

I DON'T KNOW WHY HE BOTHERED TELLING ME TO GO TO SCHOOL IF HE WAS JUST GOING TO FORGET ABOUT ME ANYWAY.

"THIS GRAIN OF SAND IS YOU, OMAR." WELL, THIS GRAIN OF SAND IS **YOU**, TALL SALAN, AND I'M KICKING YOU RIGHT IN THE FACE! RRRRRRRGGHHH!!

KICK

<HELLO! WHAT LOVELY WEATHER WE ARE HAVING!>

ARE YOU OK?

I GOT DUST IN MY EYES, THAT'S ALL.

MAYBE THIS WILL HELP. I BROUGHT YOU A PRESENT.

IT'S ALL ARRANGED. YOU CAN START SCHOOL TOMORROW...IN **YEAR SIX**.

IF YOU WANT TO, THAT IS.

35

DID I WANT TO GO TO SCHOOL?

HASSAN? DO YOU THINK...?

BUT I CAN'T GET THE WORDS OUT. AND I KNOW HE CAN'T ANSWER ME ANYWAY.

...FATUMA? WHAT DO **YOU** THINK I SHOULD DO?

I'VE BEEN THINKING A LOT ABOUT THIS, OMAR.

YOU ARE A BIG BOY NOW, AND I CAN'T MAKE THIS DECISION FOR YOU. IF IT IS GOD'S WILL THAT YOU SHOULD GO TO SCHOOL, THEN I WON'T STAND IN HIS WAY.

I THINK YOU SHOULD LOOK DEEP INSIDE YOURSELF AND SEE WHAT GOD IS TELLING YOU TO DO.

IF THIS IS GOD'S WILL, THEN HE WILL MAKE EVERYTHING OK. DON'T WORRY.

EVERYTHING WILL BE OK.

FATUMA IS ALWAYS SAYING "EVERYTHING WILL BE OK"...BUT SOMETIMES THAT'S HARD TO BELIEVE.

SOMETIMES WHEN I CAN'T SLEEP, OR WHEN SOMETHING'S BOTHERING ME...

I BARELY SLEPT THAT NIGHT, AS USUAL—BUT IT WASN'T JUST BECAUSE I WAS UNCOMFORTABLE.

...I KNOW IT SOUNDS SILLY, BUT I GO OUTSIDE AND LOOK AT THIS ONE STAR.

I DON'T REMEMBER MUCH FROM WHEN I WAS LITTLE. OR MAYBE, I DON'T HAVE MUCH I **WANT** TO REMEMBER.

I REMEMBER THIS STAR, THOUGH. MAYBE IT'S NOT EVEN A REAL MEMORY, BUT THIS STAR MAKES ME FEEL SAFE, LIKE MY MUM AND DAD ARE NEARBY. I USED TO ACTUALLY **TALK** TO THE STAR, WHICH SEEMS REALLY CHILDISH TO ME NOW. STILL, FEELING LIKE MY PARENTS ARE CLOSE MAKES IT EASIER TO MAKE BIG DECISIONS.

IF I WENT TO SCHOOL, I'D ONLY BE AWAY FROM HASSAN FOR A FEW HOURS. I'D COME RIGHT HOME.

BUT...MY MUM THOUGHT SHE WOULD COME HOME AGAIN TOO.

I FELT TORN IN HALF. SHOULD I GO TO SCHOOL? OR SHOULD I STAY WITH MY FAMILY?

I THINK I KNOW WHAT MY PARENTS WOULD SAY IF THEY COULD. THEY'D SAY MY MOST IMPORTANT JOB IS TO TAKE CARE OF MY BROTHER.

BUT WHAT IF SALAN IS RIGHT? WHAT IF **SCHOOL** IS THE BEST WAY TO TAKE CARE OF HIM?

THE TRUTH IS...I REALLY **WANT** TO GO TO SCHOOL. I WANT TO GO SO BADLY IT HURTS.

BUT I'M SCARED.

I DIDN'T HEAR AN ANSWER FROM THE STARS, OF COURSE. JUST THE FARAWAY CRY OF HYENAS.

NEITHER HASSAN NOR I SLEPT MUCH THAT NIGHT.

CHAPTER 3

LIKE EVERY MORNING, I HEAR THE CALL TO MORNING PRAYERS OVER THE LOUDSPEAKERS. IT'S EARLY, BUT TODAY I WAS ALREADY AWAKE.

I PRAY THAT I'M MAKING THE RIGHT DECISION.

I DON'T HAVE TO SAY A WORD—FATUMA UNDERSTANDS WHAT I'VE DECIDED.

I DON'T THINK HASSAN UNDERSTANDS...YET.

MAYBE FATUMA ISN'T CONVINCED ABOUT SCHOOL...BUT SHE STILL TRIES TO GIVE ME EXTRA PORRIDGE AT BREAKFAST. I'M HUNGRY, BUT I KNOW THAT EXTRA HELPING CAME FROM HER OWN PLATE, SO I LIE.

I'M TOO NERVOUS. I CAN'T EAT.

I GUESS I SHOULD GO NOW.

I'LL ONLY BE GONE FOR A FEW HOURS. FATUMA WILL TAKE CARE OF YOU. YOU'LL BE SAFE.

I LOOKED HIM IN THE EYES, AND I TRY TO USE MY MENTAL POWERS TO SEND A MESSAGE RIGHT INTO **HIS** EYES.

I'LL COME BACK. I **PROMISE**.

WAAAAAAAAAAAAAAAAA!!!!

IT WAS SO HARD TO LEAVE HASSAN. I TRIED TO SHOVE MY FEARS DEEP INSIDE ME.

BUT EVEN WITH MY BROTHER CRYING AS I WALKED AWAY, EVEN WITH FEAR GNAWING AT MY INSIDES...
A TINY PART OF ME FELT...

HAPPY.

WHAT WAS **WRONG** WITH ME?

HEY! OMAR! ARE YOU COMING TO SCHOOL WITH US? YOU DIDN'T TELL ME!

I DON'T THINK YOU'RE ALLOWED TO JUST START SCHOOL. YOU HAVE TO GET PERMISSION.

I DID GET PERMISSION, ALI. AND LOOK, I HAVE A WORKBOOK **AND** A PENCIL!

WOW!

WHERE'D YOU GET THOSE?

THAT'S NOT FAIR! YOU JUST STARTED SCHOOL! HOW COME YOU GOT A PENCIL?

DON'T LISTEN TO TALL ALI. HE'S JUST MAD BECAUSE HE KNOWS YOU'RE GOING TO GET BETTER GRADES THAN HIM.

AM NOT, LIMPY!

I WASN'T ABOUT TO SAY ANYTHING IN FRONT OF TALL ALI...BUT I SERIOUSLY DOUBTED I'D BE GETTING BETTER GRADES THAN HIM, OR ANYONE ELSE FOR THAT MATTER. I'VE NEVER BEEN TO SCHOOL BEFORE. HOW WAS I GOING TO KEEP UP WITH ALL THE OTHER KIDS?

HEY, OMAR!

HI, NIMO.

I'VE KNOWN NIMO BASICALLY MY WHOLE LIFE TOO. SHE LIVES A FEW TENTS AWAY FROM ME, WITH HER MUM AND HER TWO OLDER BROTHERS.

SHE WAS WALKING WITH MARYAM—**OF COURSE**. THEY ARE ALWAYS TOGETHER, EVEN THOUGH MARYAM'S A LITTLE OLDER. I THINK SHE'S AROUND FIFTEEN. I THINK I'M ELEVEN...BUT IT'S HARD TO KNOW FOR SURE, BECAUSE I DON'T KNOW WHEN MY BIRTHDAY IS.

MARYAM IS QUIET, LIKE ME, AND NIMO IS, WELL...

HEY, IT'S THE MOUSE AND THE SHRIMP!

...**NOT** QUIET.

MARYAM'S NOT A **MOUSE**—SHE JUST KNOWS BETTER THAN TO WASTE HER BREATH TALKING TO IDIOTS. AND I'D RATHER BE A SHRIMP THAN AN IDIOT. YOU'RE THE WORST OF BOTH WORLDS, TALL ALI...YOU'RE LIKE...A TOWERING TREE OF AN IDIOT.

HA-HA-HA! "TOWERING TREE OF AN IDIOT"!

SHUT UP.

HEY, SPEAKING OF TREES...

SNORT

...THAT'S WHERE THE SCHOOL USED TO BE, RIGHT?

WE HAVE BUILDINGS AND DESKS NOW, YOU KNOW.

I **KNOW**, I'M JUST SAYING.

BACK WHEN I FIRST ARRIVED IN DADAAB, THE CAMP WAS SO NEW THAT SCHOOLS HADN'T BEEN BUILT YET. KIDS JUST SAT UNDER A TREE WHILE TEACHERS TAUGHT THE LESSONS.

NOW THERE ARE BUILDINGS.

I WISH HASSAN WERE WITH ME. I WOULDN'T FEEL SO NERVOUS IF I HAD MY BROTHER BY MY SIDE.

GULP

COME WITH ME. I'LL SHOW YOU WHERE TO GO.

GO SIT ON THE FLOOR, ALI. LET DANTEY SIT HERE TODAY.

WHAT? BUT I...

JUST GO, OR I'LL TELL TEACHER AHMED WHAT YOU SAID ABOUT HIS EARS YESTERDAY.

USUALLY WE TAKE TURNS SITTING AT THE DESKS, BUT I'M TIRED OF THAT JERK.

THERE ARE A LOT OF KIDS HERE!

NOT MUCH ELSE TO DO AROUND HERE, IS THERE?

SOME OF THE STUDENTS HERE ARE OLDER, MAYBE FIFTEEN OR SIXTEEN YEARS OLD. KIDS HERE GO TO SCHOOL WHEN THEY CAN, SO SOMETIMES THEY GET A LATE START. ALL THE GIRLS ARE SITTING ON ONE SIDE OF THE ROOM, AND BOYS ON THE OTHER. THERE AREN'T AS MANY GIRLS AS THERE ARE BOYS.

IT SEEMS LIKE HALF THE GIRLS IN CLASS ARE HANGING AROUND NIMO'S DESK, SINGING A SONG. I'M NOT SURPRISED—SHE SINGS **ALL** THE TIME.

R-R-RING!

AAAAAAAAGH!

RELAX, THAT'S JUST THE BELL! IT'S TIME FOR ENGLISH CLASS.

<GOOD MORNING, CLASS.>

<GOOD MORNING, SIR.>

<TODAY WE ARE REVIEWING INTRODUCTIONS.>

Hello my name

WHEW MAYBE I'LL BE OK IN SCHOOL. I UNDERSTAND **THIS**!

AFTER FORTY-FIVE MINUTES, THE BELL RANG, AND A NEW TEACHER CAME IN.

NEXT IS HISTORY CLASS. THIS ONE IS REALLY BORING.

<TODAY WE'RE GOING TO STUDY THE KENYAN POLITICAL SYSTEM.>

1997

WAIT! WHY IS SHE SPEAKING IN ENGLISH? I THOUGHT THIS WAS HISTORY CLASS!

ALL OF OUR CLASSES ARE IN ENGLISH! I THOUGHT YOU KNEW THAT!

OH, CRUD.

I COULD BARELY UNDERSTAND WHAT THE TEACHER WAS SAYING! I WROTE DOWN THE WORDS I KNEW IN MY NOTEBOOK.

WE DIDN'T HAVE ANY BOOKS TO READ FROM, SO WE HAD TO LISTEN REALLY CAREFULLY TO THE TEACHER...

...WHICH WASN'T EASY WITH SO MANY KIDS CROWDED IN ONE ROOM!

WHY WON'T THEY JUST KEEP QUIET?!

MOST OF THE OTHER KIDS DIDN'T HAVE PENCILS OR PAPER. I WAS ONE OF THE FEW KIDS WHO WAS ABLE TO TAKE NOTES IN CLASS. I WROTE REALLY TINY TO TRY AND SAVE MY PAPER.

AFTER HISTORY, WE HAD SCIENCE CLASS.

AND THEN MATHS CLASS. AT LEAST THERE WOULD BE **ONE** SUBJECT I COULD UNDERSTAND.

WHEW JUST NUMBERS! I CAN DO **THIS**.

AFTER MATHS WE HAD A LUNCH BREAK. SOME OF THE KIDS WENT HOME TO EAT, BUT A LOT OF THEM STAYED TO TALK OR PLAY WITH THEIR FRIENDS.

WHY DIDN'T YOU TELL ME ALL THE CLASSES ARE IN ENGLISH?! WHY DON'T THE TEACHERS SPEAK SOMALI?!

WELL, NOT ALL THE KIDS IN THE CAMP ARE SOMALI, ARE THEY? THAT GUY IS ETHIOPIAN, THOSE KIDS OVER THERE ARE SUDANESE...EVERYONE SPEAKS DIFFERENT LANGUAGES, SO ENGLISH IS SOMETHING EVERYONE CAN UNDERSTAND.

YEAH, EVERYONE UNDERSTANDS IT EXCEPT **ME**.

ARE YOU GOING HOME TO EAT?

NAH. LET'S GO PLAY FOOTBALL WITH A REAL BALL FOR ONCE.

THE TRUTH WAS, I KNEW WE DIDN'T HAVE ANYTHING TO EAT TODAY. AND ALSO...I THOUGHT IT WOULD BE EASIER JUST TO STAY AWAY. IT WOULD BE REALLY HARD TO LEAVE HASSAN TWICE IN ONE DAY.

AFTER LUNCH, WE HAD:

ARABIC

KISWAHILI

ARTS & CRAFTS

TODAY, WE ARE GOING TO SCULPT ELEPHANTS FROM MUD. EVERYONE OUTSIDE.

JUST LIKE THE BUILDING PIT!

THEN THE FINAL BELL RANG... AND THAT WAS IT! WE DIDN'T HAVE ANY HOMEWORK—AFTER ALL, NOBODY HAD ANY BOOKS TO STUDY WITH.

THAT WAS SOOOO BORING.

MY BRAIN HURT FROM ALL THE LISTENING AND CONCENTRATING AND NEW FACTS SHOVED INSIDE IT... BUT FOR SOME REASON I COULDN'T STOP SMILING.

I'M GOING TO **SCHOOL**!

WHAT ARE YOU SMILING AT, DODO HEAD?!

WEIRDOS.

SEE YOU TOMORROW, OMAR!

I'M HO—

HOOYO! HOOYO! HOOYO! HOOYO!

HE'S BEEN LOOKING FOR YOU ALL DAY! HE JUST SAT BY THE DOOR, WAITING FOR YOU.

OK, OK! YOU CAN LET GO NOW. I'M HOME.

I MISSED YOU TOO.

I TELL HASSAN EVERYTHING I LEARNED IN SCHOOL. I TRY TO REMEMBER THE THINGS I DIDN'T PUT IN MY NOTEBOOK, AND I WRITE IT IN THE SAND. EVEN IF HE DOESN'T UNDERSTAND, I SHARE IT WITH HIM.

I CAN'T KNOW FOR SURE, OF COURSE...BUT A WARM FEELING WASHES OVER ME, LIKE I'M DOING THE RIGHT THING. I HOPE MY PARENTS WOULD BE PROUD.

CHAPTER 4

GOING TO SCHOOL IN A REFUGEE CAMP ISN'T THE EASIEST THING IN THE WORLD.

SCHOOL HERE IS...

...CHAOTIC.

THERE'S A LOT OF YELLING AND FIGHTING BECAUSE THERE ARE SO MANY KIDS. IT'S REALLY HOT, AND IT'S HARD TO CONCENTRATE. SOMETIMES KIDS FAINT AT SCHOOL BECAUSE THEY'RE SO HUNGRY. SOMETIMES THE **TEACHERS** LOOK LIKE THEY'RE GOING TO FAINT FROM HUNGER. AFTER ALL, MOST OF THEM ARE REFUGEES TOO.

BUT EVEN THOUGH IT'S LOUD, AND CROWDED, AND HOT...I LOVE IT. IT'S LIKE...MY BRAIN WAS STARVING, AND NOW IT'S GETTING THE FOOD IT NEEDS.

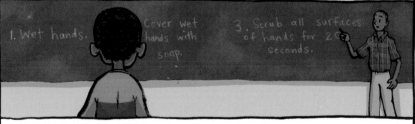

WE LEARNED ABOUT THINGS LIKE MULTIPLICATION AND DIVISION AND SPELLING, OF COURSE...BUT OUR TEACHERS ALSO TAUGHT US THINGS LIKE HOW TO WASH OUR HANDS CORRECTLY, AND WHY KIDS SHOULDN'T PLAY IN PILES OF RUBBISH.

EVERY DAY AFTER SCHOOL, AS SOON AS I GET HOME, HASSAN AND I GO OUT FOR A LONG WALK. HE HATES BEING COOPED UP ALL DAY—HE DOESN'T GET TO PLAY MUCH WITH FATUMA. I TRY TO TELL HIM THAT I'M GOING TO SCHOOL TO HELP HIM...BUT I DON'T THINK HE UNDERSTANDS. HE JUST KNOWS THAT I'M GONE.

EVERY NIGHT WHEN WE ATE SUPPER, I'D TELL FATUMA AND HASSAN WHAT I LEARNED IN SCHOOL THAT DAY.

MY TEACHER SAID SOME PEOPLE THINK IT'S NOT IMPORTANT FOR GIRLS TO GO TO SCHOOL, BUT HE SAID THAT'S WRONG.

YOU KNOW, WHEN I WAS A LITTLE GIRL IN SOMALIA, I NEVER WENT TO SCHOOL.

MY EARS PERKED UP. FATUMA HARDLY EVER TALKED ABOUT HER LIFE BACK IN SOMALIA.

I LIVED IN A VERY RURAL VILLAGE. THE ONLY SCHOOL WAS FAR AWAY, AND I HAD NO BROTHERS TO PROTECT ME. IT WAS VERY DANGEROUS FOR A GIRL TO WALK ALL THAT WAY BY HERSELF.

AND THE GIRLS IN MY VILLAGE WHO **DID** HAVE BROTHERS USUALLY STAYED HOME TO DO CHORES WHILE THE BOYS WENT TO SCHOOL.

I WAS NEVER TOLD THAT SCHOOL WAS IMPORTANT...BUT MAYBE SALAN IS RIGHT. MAYBE TIMES ARE CHANGING, AND I NEED TO CHANGE WITH THEM.

EVERYTHING IS DIFFERENT NOW.

NIMO AND MARYAM ARE IN MY CLASS. THEY SEEM TO LIKE GOING TO SCHOOL.

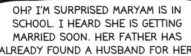

OH? I'M SURPRISED MARYAM IS IN SCHOOL. I HEARD SHE IS GETTING MARRIED SOON. HER FATHER HAS ALREADY FOUND A HUSBAND FOR HER.

MARYAM'S GETTING **MARRIED**?

IT WAS WEIRD TO THINK THAT SOMEONE I KNEW WAS GETTING **MARRIED** ALREADY. QUIET MARYAM, WHO BARELY TALKED AT ALL.

I DIDN'T KNOW WHAT TO SAY TO THAT... SO I DIDN'T SAY ANYTHING.

THE NEXT DAY I PAID MORE ATTENTION TO MARYAM AND THE OTHER GIRLS IN MY CLASS. SOME OF THE GIRLS WERE TALKING AND JOKING AROUND... BUT NOT MARYAM. HER EYES WERE GLUED TO THE TEACHER. SHE ALWAYS GOT THE ANSWER RIGHT WHEN THE TEACHER CALLED ON HER.

WHEN IT WAS TIME FOR LUNCH, NEITHER MARYAM NOR ANY OF THE OTHER GIRLS STAYED AT SCHOOL— THEY ALL HURRIED OFF.

WHY DON'T THE GIRLS STAY AT SCHOOL FOR LUNCH, DO YOU THINK?

I DUNNO. THEY PROBABLY HAVE TO GO HOME TO PREPARE LUNCH FOR THEIR FAMILIES.

C'MON, LET'S GO PLAY FOOTBALL.

MAYBE THINGS HAVEN'T CHANGED AS MUCH AS FATUMA THOUGHT.

55

I STARTED NOTICING THAT WHEN I'D FETCH WATER BEFORE SCHOOL I'D SEE SOME OF MY CLASSMATES THERE TOO...BUT ONLY THE GIRLS.

WHEN I WENT FOR WALKS WITH HASSAN AFTER SCHOOL, I'D SEE OTHER KIDS WATCHING THEIR SIBLINGS TOO...BUT ONLY THE GIRLS.

BESIDES NIMO AND MARYAM, NONE OF THE OTHER GIRLS IN MY BLOCK EVEN **WENT** TO SCHOOL—THEY STAYED HOME TO DO CHORES.

IT DIDN'T SEEM FAIR THAT THE GIRLS HAD TO DO ALL THE WORK WHILE THEIR BROTHERS GOT TO PLAY. SINCE I DON'T HAVE ANY SISTERS, AND FATUMA IS SO OLD—**I** DID A LOT OF THE CHORES AT HOME. SOME BOYS MADE FUN OF ME FOR THAT.

HEY, DANTEY! WHERE'S YOUR DRESS?

AFTER A FEW WEEKS OF DOING ALL THE CHORES, TAKING CARE OF HASSAN, AND GOING TO SCHOOL, I REALISED HOW EXHAUSTED NIMO AND MARYAM AND THE OTHER GIRLS MUST BE.

HOW DO THEY **DO** IT?!

RRRRRRGHHHH! HASSAN! YOU HAVE TO TELL ME IF YOU NEED TO USE THE TOILET! NOW I HAVE TO WASH YOUR CLOTHES **AGAIN**...I'LL HAVE TO FETCH MORE WATER...

GO ON. TAKE YOUR CLOTHES OFF!

I'M SORRY, HASSAN. I'M JUST SO TIRED. I CAN'T DO ALL THIS.

IT'S TOO HARD.

HELLO! OMAR, HOW IS SCHOOL GOING?

THAT BAD, HUH?

SALAN, IT'S TOO HARD! I HAVE TO WATCH HASSAN, I HAVE TO DO ALL THE CLEANING, I HAVE TO FETCH THE WATER...AND EVERYTHING IN SCHOOL IS IN ENGLISH, SO I BARELY UNDERSTAND ANYTHING ANYWAY! WHAT'S THE POINT OF GOING TO SCHOOL? MAYBE I SHOULD JUST GIVE UP.

HMMM. WELL, I CAN'T HELP WITH YOUR CHORES, BUT... YOU DO KNOW THAT I RUN A PRIVATE SCHOOL, YES? OFFERING ENGLISH LESSONS? WHY DON'T YOU STOP BY TOMORROW AFTER CLASS AND WE'LL SEE IF WE CAN CATCH YOU UP ON YOUR ENGLISH?

HOW MUCH DOES **THAT** COST?

HOW ABOUT YOU FETCH WATER FOR MY SCHOOL ONCE A WEEK AND WE CALL IT EVEN?

WHAT I **THOUGHT** WAS:

GREAT. **MORE** LESSONS AND CHORES.

WHAT I **SAID** WAS:

THANK YOU, SIR.

...SO MAYBE I WASN'T READY TO GIVE UP ON SCHOOL **JUST** YET.

NOW MY NEW SCHEDULE WAS: FETCH **MORE** WATER EARLY IN THE MORNING. GO TO SCHOOL. GO TO AFTER-SCHOOL ENGLISH LESSONS. GO HOME TO HASSAN, WHO WAS NOT HAPPY I WAS GONE EVEN LONGER, AND NOW HAD TO DO CHORES INSTEAD OF PLAY. GO TO BED.

AFTER A FEW WEEKS, MY ENGLISH WAS MUCH BETTER...BUT I WAS **SO TIRED**.

ARE YOU TWO... STUDYING? **NOW?!** THE SUN'S BARELY UP!

NO REST FOR THE WEARY! BESIDES, WE HAVE BIG PLANS, DON'T WE, MARYAM? YES INDEED, BIG PLANS.

NIMO OBVIOUSLY WANTED ME TO ASK ABOUT HER "BIG PLANS"...BUT I WAS TOO EXHAUSTED.

THEY MUST REALLY LOVE SCHOOL IF THEY'RE STUDYING THIS EARLY IN THE MORNING. BUT I COULDN'T HELP WONDERING...

...WHY WAS MARYAM STUDYING SO HARD IF SHE WAS JUST GOING TO GET MARRIED SOON ANYWAY?

CHAPTER 5

OMAR, ARE YOU ALL RIGHT? YOU DON'T LOOK SO GOOD.

I'VE BEEN AT SCHOOL FOR ALMOST TWO MONTHS NOW. I'VE BEEN GETTING LESS SLEEP AT NIGHT, AND...I DON'T KNOW WHY, MAYBE IT'S THE LONG WALK TO SCHOOL...BUT THESE DAYS I AM HUNGRY. **ALL. THE. TIME.** I MEAN, YOU'RE ALWAYS HUNGRY IN A REFUGEE CAMP...BUT THESE PAST FEW WEEKS HAVE BEEN PARTICULARY BAD.

YOU LOOK WEAK. DO YOU NEED TO STAY HOME AND REST TODAY?

NO. I'M GOING TO SCHOOL.

I MAY BE HUNGRY ALL THE TIME, BUT AT LEAST MY BRAIN IS GETTING FULL. AND SCHOOL IS A DISTRACTION FROM THE HUNGER.

. ON SOME DAYS—DAYS LIKE TODAY— **EVERYONE** IS GRUMPY.

QUIT BREATHING ON ME!

WELL, EXCUSE ME FOR BEING **ALIVE!**

ON DAYS LIKE TODAY, SOME KIDS JUST DON'T COME TO CLASS. THREE KIDS FAINTED THIS MORNING ALREADY. IT HAPPENS EVERY TWO WEEKS LIKE CLOCKWORK. BECAUSE EVERY TWO WEEKS, WE HAVE THE **EMPTY DAYS**.

WHAT ARE THE EMPTY DAYS? WELL...

WHEN YOU'RE A REFUGEE, YOU GET FOOD EVERY FIFTEEN DAYS FROM THE DISTRIBUTION CENTRE. FOR ABOUT THE FIRST TEN DAYS IT'S OK, AND EVERYONE EATS.

BUT THE FOOD WE'RE GIVEN IS NEVER ENOUGH. DURING THE LAST FIVE DAYS, THE FOOD STARTS TO RUN OUT. AND...EVERYONE...IS...HUNGRY.

LUCKILY, TOMORROW IS DISTRIBUTION DAY. WHEN I THINK ABOUT THAT FOOD, I CAN BARELY WALK HOME, MY LEGS FEEL SO WEAK.

I HOPE THAT SOME MIRACLE HAS OCCURRED WHILE I WAS AWAY, AND THAT WE'LL HAVE SOMETHING TO EAT FOR DINNER, BUT...

HAVE SOME TEA. IT WILL HELP THE HUNGER GO AWAY.

WE RAN OUT OF TEA—I HAD TO USE TREE BARK INSTEAD.

IT'S...GOOD. THANK YOU, FATUMA.

BLECH.

HASSAN DOESN'T QUITE UNDERSTAND ABOUT THE FOOD. HE'S LIKE THE LITTLE KIDS WHO LIVE NEXT DOOR—SOMETIMES I SEE THEM HITTING THEIR MUM BECAUSE THEY'RE SO ANGRY ABOUT BEING HUNGRY. THEIR MUM DOESN'T GET MAD OR PUNISH THEM. SHE JUST LOOKS SAD AND SAYS TO THEM:

I'M SORRY, BABY. I'M SORRY.

THE LITTLE KIDS DON'T UNDERSTAND WHAT THE OLDER KIDS DO—THERE **IS** NO FOOD.

ONCE THEY ARE OLDER, THEY'LL GET USED TO BEING HUNGRY.

HAVE YOU EVER TRIED TO SLEEP WITH AN EMPTY STOMACH, ON A WOVEN MAT ON THE DIRT? WELL, TAKE IT FROM ME, IT'S NOT EASY. HASSAN AND I KEPT TOSSING AND TURNING, EVEN MORE THAN USUAL.

WE WOKE UP THE NEXT MORNING AND HAD SOME DISGUSTING BARK TEA. BELIEVE IT OR NOT, IT'S BETTER THAN NOTHING.

THEN I GOT MY RATION CARD FROM THE SECRET HIDING PLACE IN MY TENT.

EVERY FAMILY IN DADAAB HAS A CARD LIKE THIS—THE UN GIVES IT TO YOU WHEN YOU REGISTER AS A REFUGEE. MY CARD IS PUNCHED IN AT TWO: THAT MEANS IT'S GOOD FOR TWO PEOPLE—ME AND HASSAN. EVERY TIME WE GET A NEW RATION, A HOLE IS PUNCHED IN THE CARD. ONCE THE CARD IS FULL, WE GET A NEW ONE.

I WEAR MINE ON A STRING AROUND MY NECK.

FATUMA ALREADY LEFT TO GET HER RATIONS—SHE LIKES TO GO WITH HER FRIENDS SO THEY CAN GOSSIP WHILE THEY'RE WAITING IN LINE. THERE IS A **LOT** OF WAITING IN LINE.

THERE'S ONLY ONE FOOD DISTRIBUTION CENTRE FOR ALL OF IFO. SO PEOPLE FROM ALL OVER THE CAMP COME TO ONE PLACE FOR THE DAY.

THERE ARE A LOT OF PEOPLE IN THIS CAMP. AND MORE AND MORE PEOPLE ARE ARRIVING EVERY DAY.

ON DAYS LIKE TODAY, IT REALLY SINKS IN JUST HOW **BIG** DADAAB IS. HUGE CROWDS. THOUSANDS OF PEOPLE. MAYBE YOU'LL SEE SOMEONE IN THE CROWD YOU RECOGNISE, AND YOU DIDN'T EVEN REALISE THEY WERE HERE.

GASP!

HASSAN! FOLLOW ME! HURRY! HURRY! PUT THAT DOWN, COME ON!

COME ON! HURRY!

MAYBE YOU'LL SEE SOMEONE YOU'VE BEEN LOOKING FOR.

SOMEONE WHO HAS BEEN SEARCHING FOR YOU, BUT SHE DIDN'T KNOW WHERE TO FIND YOU...

MAMA?

HOOYO?

CAN I HELP YOU?
OH. I...I'M SORRY. I THOUGHT YOU WERE SOMEONE ELSE.
DID YOU LOSE YOUR MAMA? YOU SHOULDN'T RUN OFF FROM HER IN THE MARKET—YOU SHOULD STICK CLOSE TO HER. COME ON, HALIMA.
I CAN'T BELIEVE I THOUGHT IT WAS HER. I'M SO STUPID.

IT'S STUPID TO KEEP LOOKING FOR HER. POINTLESS. IF SHE WERE IN THIS CAMP, SHE'D HAVE FOUND US BY NOW. IF SHE WERE ALIVE **ANYWHERE**, SHE'D HAVE FOUND US. A MUM WOULDN'T ABANDON HER KIDS.

WOULD SHE?

I WISH THERE WEREN'T SO MUCH TIME TO THINK IN A REFUGEE CAMP. BUT I HAVE NOTHING TO DO TODAY BUT

WAIT...

WAIT...

WAIT.

I TRY TO FORGET. I **WANT** TO FORGET.

STUPID. STUPID. STUPID.

WE GET IN A DIFFERENT LINE FOR EACH RATION. THE FOOD WE RECEIVE TODAY IS:

MAIZE

COOKING OIL

SALT

SOMETIMES WE GET FLOUR... BUT NOT TODAY.

IT'S NOT HARD FOR ME TO CARRY THE FOOD HOME, BECAUSE THE BAG'S NOT HEAVY.

WHEN WE GET HOME, WE GIVE OUR FOOD RATIONS TO FATUMA. BECAUSE SHE COOKS FOR US, SHE KEEPS THE FOOD SAFE IN HER TENT. PLUS, SINCE SHE'S USUALLY HOME, SHE CAN MAKE SURE NO ONE STEALS IT.

SEE? EVERYTHING SEEMS BETTER WITH A LITTLE BIT OF FOOD. EVERYTHING WILL BE OK.

YOU KEEP SAYING THAT! IT ISN'T **TRUE!** **NOTHING IS OK!**

R-R-RRRRRGH!!!

SOB

WHY DID SHE LEAVE US? WHY DIDN'T SHE COME WITH US?

FATUMA DOESN'T GET MAD OR PUNISH ME. SHE JUST LOOKS SAD AND SAYS TO ME:

I'M SORRY, BABY. I'M SORRY.

69

CHAPTER 6

SCHOOL IS A GOOD DISTRACTION FROM MY WORRIES.

TOO SOON, HOWEVER, THE SEMESTER IS OVER AND WE HAVE A ONE-MONTH BREAK. MAYBE IN SOME PLACES KIDS LOOK FORWARD TO BREAKS FROM SCHOOL...BUT NOT ME. I DIDN'T WANT TO GO BACK TO THOSE LONG, EMPTY DAYS, WITH TOO MUCH TIME TO THINK.

HEY, COME ON— LET'S LOOK AT THE LIST!

AT THE END OF THE SEMESTER, THE TEACHER POSTS THE RANKING OF ALL THE STUDENTS BASED ON THEIR SCORES ON EXAMS. I WAS SCARED TO LOOK—I FIGURED I WOULD BE AT THE VERY BOTTOM, BUT...

HEY, NUMBER THIRTY-THREE! THAT'S NOT SO BAD!

NOT SO GREAT, EITHER. EVEN TALL ALI DID BETTER THAN YOU.

HA-HA. AND WHAT ARE YOU, NUMBER TEN, GENIUS?

NO. NUMBER TWELVE. BUT WHATEVER.

NUMBER TWELVE WAS REALLY, REALLY GOOD. BUT I WASN'T JEALOUS. I HAD JUST STARTED SCHOOL. I HAD TIME TO GET BETTER.

THE GIRLS HAVE A SEPARATE LIST FROM THE BOYS.

WOW! MARYAM, YOU'RE THE NUMBER ONE GIRL?! CONGRATULATIONS!

THANKS, OMAR.

OF **COURSE** SHE'S NUMBER ONE! SHE'S THE SMARTEST GIRL IN OUR WHOLE CLASS, PROBABLY IN THE WHOLE CAMP! EVERYONE KNOWS THAT!

YOU PROBABLY CHEATED OFF HER, NIMO—THAT'S HOW COME YOU'RE NUMBER TWO GIRL.

SHUT UP, AMINA! YOU'RE JUST JEALOUS BECAUSE YOU'RE, WHAT, NUMBER SEVENTEEN? I DIDN'T KNOW WE HAD SEVENTEEN GIRLS IN CLASS. MY **GOAT** COULD'VE DONE BETTER THAN YOU.

COME ON, NIMO. YOU DON'T WANT TO GET IN A FIGHT ON THE LAST DAY OF SCHOOL!

YEAH, LET'S GO! IT'S HOLIDAY TIME!

OK, SO MAYBE THERE WERE A **FEW** GOOD THINGS ABOUT NO SCHOOL.

SINCE WE DIDN'T HAVE TO WAKE UP QUITE SO EARLY THE NEXT MORNING, SOME OF THE KIDS IN A2 DECIDED TO PLAY NIGHTTIME HIDE-AND-SEEK.

THE FIRST STEP IN PLAYING NIGHTTIME HIDE-AND-SEEK IS WAITING

UNTIL

IT GETS

REALLY

DARK.

C'MON! OVER HERE!

SINCE THERE'S NO ELECTRICITY IN THE CAMP, IT GETS **SUPER** DARK. YOU CAN BASICALLY STAND IN THE MIDDLE OF A FIELD AND NO ONE WILL SEE YOU!

SOMETIMES YOU'RE WAITING A LONG TIME TO BE FOUND.

WHERE **IS** EVERYBODY?

SO WHAT DID YOUR PARENTS SAY ABOUT THE SCHOOL RESULTS? ABOUT YOU BEING NUMBER TWELVE?

MY MUM WAS HAPPY. MY DAD ISN'T HOME, HE'S AT THE UN OFFICE.

I GOT A SINKING FEELING IN MY STOMACH.

DID HE GET NEWS ON YOUR CASE? ARE YOU GOING TO AMERICA?

NAH. BUT...LISTEN, DON'T TELL ANYONE THIS. HE HAS A FRIEND WHO KNOWS SOMEONE AT THE UN. MY DAD JUST GAVE HIM 100 SHILLINGS TO GET OUR PAPERWORK PUSHED TO THE TOP OF THE PILE. SO IT SHOULD BE ANY TIME NOW.

WHERE'D HE GET 100 SHILLINGS?!?

HE BORROWED IT. HE SAID IT'D BE NO PROBLEM TO REPAY IT. ONCE YOU'RE IN AMERICA, YOU CAN FIND A JOB AND EARN GOOD MONEY.

OH.

I DIDN'T WANT TO THINK ABOUT JERI GOING TO AMERICA WHILE I STAYED HERE. BUT I DIDN'T HAVE 100 SHILLINGS, AND I WOULD **NEVER** HAVE 100 SHILLINGS. THERE WAS NO CHANCE FOR ME AND HASSAN TO BE RESETTLED.

SHHHHH! I HEAR SOMEONE COMING!

HASSAN! STAY REALLY QUIET, OK? DON'T SAY A WORD!

HOOYO!

TAG. YOU'RE IT.

WE PLAY A LOT OF GAMES DURING THE SCHOOL BREAK. FOR ONE THING, IT FILLS UP THE TIME SO YOU DON'T HAVE HOURS AND HOURS TO THINK ABOUT YOUR PROBLEMS. IT ALMOST HELPED ME FORGET THAT JERI WAS GOING TO GO TO AMERICA, AND I'D BE ALL ALONE HERE.

C'MON! WE'RE ALL GOING DOWN TO THE FIELD TO PLAY KABTA BILATOY!

KABTA BILATOY IS MY FAVOURITE GAME. "KABTA" IS THE SOMALI WORD FOR SANDAL. SO ONE KID TAKES OFF HIS SANDAL, AND EACH TEAM PICKS A SIDE OF THE SANDAL— HEADS OR TAILS. THEN YOU TOSS THE SANDAL IN THE AIR. IF IT LANDS HEADS UP, THEN THAT TEAM RUNS TO THE OTHER TEAM'S GOAL AND TRIES NOT TO GET TAGGED.

HASSAN ALWAYS COMES ALONG WHEN WE'RE PLAYING A GAME. HE DOESN'T UNDERSTAND THE RULES— HE JUST WANTS TO JOIN IN AND PLAY LIKE ALL THE OTHER KIDS.

BUT WHEN I TRY AND LET HIM PLAY...

...IT CAN END IN DISASTER.

THAT'S MY SHOE! GET BACK HERE!

HASSAN JUST THINKS WE'RE PLAYING A BIG GAME.

HASSAN! QUIT JOKING AROUND! COME BACK!

I AM GOING TO KILL HIM. I DON'T KNOW WHY YOU LET HIM PLAY IN THE FIRST PLACE!

HASSAN!

GRAB

LET GO, YOU IDIOT! IT'S NOT FUNNY!

STOP! DON'T HURT HIM!

SHOVE

I DON'T KNOW WHY YOU BOTHER TAKING CARE OF THIS MORON! HE'S A WASTE OF SPACE. YOU SHOULD LET HIM WANDER OFF INTO THE BUSH TO GET EATEN BY LIONS!

STOP IT, ALI. JUST STOP.

NOW I KNOW WHY YOU'RE ORPHANS. THAT'S PROBABLY WHY YOUR MUM LEFT YOU— I'D RATHER BE DEAD TOO, THAN—

AAAAARGH!!
SHUT UP! JUST **SHUT UP**!
HEY! KNOCK IT OFF, YOU HOODLUMS! YOU'RE DRIVING AWAY MY CUSTOMERS!
STOP! ALI, GET OUT OF HERE, YOU BIG JERK! TAKE YOUR STUPID SANDAL! COME ON, DANTEY, LET'S GO.
OW! LET **GO** OF ME! I HAVE TO STOP FOR A MINUTE.

THE TRUTH IS...I WORRY ALL THE TIME ABOUT HASSAN AND HIS FUTURE. I KNOW THAT LOTS OF PEOPLE THINK LIKE TALL ALI. SOME PEOPLE JUST AREN'T KIND TO SOMEONE WITH DISABILITIES AROUND HERE.

I DON'T KNOW HOW SOME PEOPLE CAN BE SO CRUEL.

HERE, HASSAN. WIPE YOUR NOSE ON MY SHIRT. IT'S OK—IT'S TIME TO WASH THIS SHIRT ANYWAY.

YOU KNOW, I REALLY HATED IT WHEN EVERYONE STARTED CALLING ME "JERI". IT REMINDED ME THAT I WAS DIFFERENT FROM EVERYONE ELSE.

I DIDN'T KNOW THAT! I COULD CALL YOU SOMETHING ELSE...

I WASN'T FINISHED.

BUT NOW...I DON'T MIND THE NAME SO MUCH. I MEAN, IT'S PART OF WHO I AM. I LIMP. BUT IT'S ONLY **PART** OF WHO I AM.

SHAME WASHED OVER ME. I'M ALWAYS THINKING ABOUT ME AND HASSAN AND **OUR** PROBLEMS. I FORGET OTHER PEOPLE HAVE THEIR OWN STRUGGLES TO DEAL WITH.

THERE ARE LOTS OF JERKS LIKE TALL ALI AND...WELL, **OTHER** PEOPLE...WHO THINK I CAN'T DO ANYTHING BECAUSE I LIMP. BUT THEY'RE **WRONG**.

I DO REALLY WELL IN MY EXAMS AT SCHOOL. BETTER THAN TALL ALI. AND **SOMEDAY** MY DAD WILL SEE THAT IS WORTH SOMETHING.

SO YOU CAN'T LISTEN TO PEOPLE LIKE TALL ALI WHEN THEY SAY MEAN THINGS.

YOU KNOW, HASSAN ISN'T HELPLESS, EITHER. THERE ARE LOTS OF THINGS HE CAN DO, EVEN WITH A DISABILITY.

I KNOW, JERI. I KNOW HAVING A DISABILITY DOESN'T MAKE YOU HELPLESS.

IT'S JUST...YOU KIND OF **BABY** HIM SOMETIMES, JUST LIKE PEOPLE BABY ME. AND HASSAN **ISN'T** A BABY. HE TAKES CARE OF ANIMALS, AND HE HELPS YOUR NEIGHBOURS.

JUST...DON'T UNDERESTIMATE HIM. RIGHT, HASSAN?

BUT LIFE IS STILL GOING TO BE HARD FOR HIM. DON'T YOU EVER GET MAD? DON'T YOU EVER THINK THAT YOUR LIFE WOULD BE **EASIER** IF YOU DIDN'T HAVE A DISABILITY?

SOMETIMES.

LOOK...I DIDN'T **ASK** FOR THIS LIMP. BUT I DIDN'T ASK TO LIVE IN A REFUGEE CAMP EITHER. BUT HERE WE ARE, RIGHT?

I GUESS YOU JUST HAVE TO TRY TO APPRECIATE THE GOOD PARTS AND MAKE THE MOST OUT OF WHAT YOU'VE GOT.

COME ON. LET'S GO HOME.

OVER THE NEXT FEW DAYS, I TOOK JERI'S ADVICE. I TOOK HASSAN WITH ME TO COLLECT FIREWOOD, AND HE HELPED ME CARRY WATER AND SWEEP UP.

I'M SORRY, HASSAN. I'LL TRY TO DO BETTER.

HASSAN SEEMED TO LIKE THESE CHORES, AND HE WAS GOOD AT THEM. MAYBE JERI WAS RIGHT—MAYBE I **WAS** UNDERESTIMATING MY BROTHER.

ONE DAY WHILE WE WERE DOING CHORES, FATUMA FELL INTO ONE OF HER QUIET SPELLS. FATUMA IS ALWAYS QUIET...BUT SOMETIMES SHE DOESN'T TALK AT **ALL**. SHE JUST SITS AND STARES OFF INTO SPACE, LIKE SHE IS SEEING A GHOST. SHE CAN STAY THIS WAY FOR **HOURS**.

I'VE LEARNED TO GIVE HER SOME TIME ALONE WHEN THIS HAPPENS.

COME ON, HASSAN. LET'S GO FOR A WALK.

USUALLY WHEN WE WENT FOR WALKS, WE'D GO BY THE NEW ARRIVAL AREA TO SCAN THE CROWDS. FOR **HER**. BUT I DIDN'T FEEL LIKE DOING THAT RIGHT NOW.

EVER SINCE THAT DAY I THOUGHT I SAW MY MUM...I'VE BEEN KIND OF **MAD** AT HER. WHICH OF COURSE IS TOTALLY STUPID. HOW CAN YOU BE IN A FIGHT WITH SOMEONE WHO'S NOT EVEN HERE?

INSTEAD, WE ENDED UP...

HI, NIMO.

HEY, OMAR! HI, HASSAN! COME ON IN! MARYAM IS HERE TOO.

NIMO'S FAMILY IS ONE OF THE WEALTHIER ONES IN OUR BLOCK. THAT'S WHY THEY'RE ABLE TO HAVE THESE STURDY FENCES AND REAL WALLS ON THEIR HOUSE. AND GOATS!

NIMO'S MUM IS REALLY NICE. SHE WEAVES BASKETS TO SELL IN THE MARKET, AND SHE ALWAYS TELLS STORIES TO US KIDS WHILE SHE'S WEAVING.

OMAR, HASSAN! COME JOIN US!

SHE SAYS SOMALIA IS A NATION OF POETS, AND IT'S IMPORTANT TO KEEP THE OLD STORIES AND SONGS ALIVE.

NNNN! NNNN!

OH, I KNOW. YOU WANT TO SEE THE GOATS, DO YOU? COME ON, THEN.

HASSAN LOVES NIMO'S GOATS. SOMETIMES I THINK HE LOVES THEM MORE THAN ME.

HOW'S YOUR HOLIDAY GOING, OMAR?

IT'S OK, I...HEY!

82

ARE YOU TWO **STUDYING**? IT'S THE **HOLIDAYS**! AND YOU'RE NUMBERS ONE AND TWO IN THE CLASS— YOU DON'T NEED TO STUDY NOW!

HOW DO YOU THINK WE GOT TO NUMBERS ONE AND TWO IN THE CLASS? IT TAKES A LOT OF WORK TO STAY AT THE TOP!

BUT... **WHY**? YOU DON'T HAVE TO BE THE VERY BEST IN CLASS.

IF YOU'RE JUST GOING TO GET MARRIED SOON ANYWAY, I THINK...BUT DON'T SAY.

LISTEN...CAN YOU KEEP A SECRET?

NO! DON'T TELL HIM!

OH, IT'S JUST DANTEY. HE WON'T TELL ANYONE. WILL YOU, DANTEY?

NIMO DIDN'T WAIT FOR AN ANSWER. SHE JUST PULLED SOMETHING OUT OF HER POCKET AND HANDED IT TO ME.

CANADA? SO? YOU WANT TO BE RESETTLED THERE BY THE UN?

NO. WE'RE GOING TO **EARN** OUR WAY TO CANADA. LAST YEAR OUR TEACHER PULLED ALL THE GIRLS ASIDE AFTER CLASS AND TOLD US THAT EVERY YEAR, THE TOP STUDENTS IN KENYA CAN EARN SCHOLARSHIPS TO STUDY AT A UNIVERSITY IN CANADA. REFUGEE KIDS TOO! AND GIRLS CAN GET EXTRA HELP, SINCE IT'S HARDER FOR US TO GO TO SCHOOL HERE. HE GAVE EACH OF US THIS PICTURE TO KEEP, AS INSPIRATION.

MARYAM AND I ARE GOING TO GET THOSE SCHOLARSHIPS, AND WE'LL GO TO THE SAME UNIVERSITY, AND WE'LL LIVE IN THE SAME HOUSE. HER FAMILY WILL LIVE ON ONE SIDE OF THE HOUSE, AND MY FAMILY WILL LIVE ON THE OTHER SIDE OF THE HOUSE. BUT WE'LL SHARE A BEDROOM, WON'T WE, MARYAM? WITH GREEN WALLS.

BLUE WALLS.

HALF GREEN, HALF BLUE. WE JUST HAVE TO STAY AT THE TOP OF OUR CLASS THROUGH SECONDARY SCHOOL, AND WE CAN GO!

DO YOU THINK YOU CAN DO IT? STAY AT THE TOP OF THE CLASS, I MEAN?

USUALLY MARYAM HAS HER HEAD DOWN LOW, BUT NOT NOW.

THAT WON'T BE A PROBLEM.

MARYAM...
I HEARD... YOU'RE GETTING MARRIED SOON. WON'T YOU HAVE TO LEAVE SCHOOL?

WELL...THAT'S WHY I'M STUDYING SO HARD.

MY PLAN IS...IF I STAY NUMBER ONE IN MY CLASS...AND DO **REALLY** WELL IN MY EXAMS AT THE END OF THE YEAR...MY DAD WILL **HAVE** TO LET ME STAY IN SCHOOL. HE'LL SEE THAT A SCHOLARSHIP TO CANADA IS WORTH A LOT MORE MONEY THAN ME GETTING MARRIED.

DON'T WORRY. I KNOW IT'LL WORK. IT **HAS** TO WORK. I CAN'T GO TO CANADA WITHOUT YOU!

I BET YOU TWO CAN DO IT. AFTER ALL, YOU'RE STUDYING DURING **THE HOLIDAYS**!

SO, WHAT ARE YOU TWO GOING TO BE? AFTER YOU GET TO CANADA?

I'M GOING TO BE AN ACTRESS AND A SINGER. OR A DOCTOR. I HAVEN'T DECIDED YET.

I'M GOING TO GO TO LAW SCHOOL IN CANADA, BUT THEN I'M GOING TO COME BACK HERE TO DADAAB. I'LL HELP REFUGEE GIRLS KNOW THEIR RIGHTS.

LISTEN, I ADMIRE YOUR SPIRIT, BUT I STILL THINK YOU'RE NUTS. WHO WOULD EVER WANT TO LEAVE CANADA AND COME BACK TO THIS PLACE?!

OH, HUSH. WHAT ABOUT YOU, OMAR? WHAT DO **YOU** WANT TO DO WHEN YOU GROW UP?

I ALWAYS THOUGHT I WANTED TO GO BACK TO SOMALIA AND BECOME A FARMER.

BUT MAYBE I WANT TO BE A SOCIAL WORKER SO I CAN HELP OTHER REFUGEES. LIFE IS HARD AROUND HERE FOR A LOT OF PEOPLE.

...I GUESS I HAVEN'T DECIDED YET EITHER.

IT WAS NICE TALKING LIKE THIS. PRETENDING WE WERE NORMAL KIDS, WITH NORMAL FUTURES TO LOOK FORWARD TO.

WE SPENT A LOT OF THE REST OF THE HOLIDAYS WITH MARYAM AND NIMO. I ALWAYS THOUGHT MARYAM WAS SO QUIET, BUT SHE WAS REALLY EASY TO TALK TO ONCE YOU GOT TO KNOW HER. ONE DAY SHE EVEN SURPRISED ME AND HASSAN WITH A GIFT.

CLOSE YOUR EYES— BOTH OF YOU!

HERE, I'LL HELP!

AND... OPEN THEM!

IT'S A...WELL, IT'S A REALLY NICE, UH...

IT'S A **SWING**! I MADE IT OUT OF PLASTIC BAGS. I MADE IT FOR **YOU**, HASSAN. I KNOW YOU LIKE TO BE OUTSIDE. NOW YOU AND MY BROTHERS AND SISTER CAN PLAY TOGETHER!

MARYAM WAS RIGHT—HASSAN LOVED THE SWING. HE SEEMED TO LOVE MARYAM'S LITTLE SIBLINGS TOO—AND THEY LOVED **HIM**.

I GUESS I HAVEN'T SEEN MY BROTHER AROUND LITTLE KIDS TOO OFTEN—BECAUSE I'M SURPRISED BY HOW GENTLE AND CARING HE IS WITH THE LITTLE ONES...

...EVEN WHEN THEY WON'T LEAVE HIM ALONE.

I THOUGHT I KNEW EVERYTHING THERE WAS TO KNOW ABOUT MY BROTHER. I THOUGHT I WAS HELPING HIM AND KEEPING HIM SAFE BY SHIELDING HIM FROM NEW PEOPLE.

BUT I THINK JERI WAS RIGHT. MAYBE I DON'T KNOW EVERYTHING ABOUT HASSAN AFTER ALL.

WHILE HASSAN AND THE LITTLE KIDS PLAYED, I STUDIED WITH NIMO AND MARYAM. SOMETIMES JERI JOINED US TOO. I HAD MY NOTES FROM CLASS, BUT MARYAM WAS LIKE A LIVING TEXTBOOK. IT'S LIKE...SHE COULD TAKE A PICTURE WITH HER BRAIN AND JUST READ IT BACK TO US.

I TOLD YOU SHE'S A GENIUS.

ACTUALLY, THE GOVERNMENT OF KENYA WAS **FORMED** IN 1963, BUT IT DIDN'T BECOME A **REPUBLIC** UNTIL 1964.

WHEN WE GOT TIRED OF STUDYING, SOMETIMES NIMO WOULD SING. SHE HAS A REALLY NICE VOICE. THE LITTLE KIDS LOVED WHEN SHE SANG.

I'VE NEVER HEARD THAT SONG BEFORE.

MARYAM WROTE IT! SHE'S A POET TOO. WHEN WE GO TO CANADA, SHE'S GOING TO WRITE SONGS AND I'M GOING TO PERFORM THEM. OR MAYBE SHE'LL WRITE PLAYS AND I'LL BE THE ACTRESS.

MARYAM, I THOUGHT YOU WERE GOING TO BE A LAWYER!

I CAN DO BOTH. I'M MULTI-TALENTED, YOU KNOW.

THE HOLIDAYS SEEMED TO GO ON AND ON, AND I COULDN'T SPEND ALL MY TIME WITH JERI, NIMO, AND MARYAM—THEY HAD OTHER THINGS THEY HAD TO DO. I DIDN'T FEEL LIKE PLAYING GAMES WITH THE OTHER A2 BOYS, SO AFTER THE CHORES WERE DONE, HASSAN AND I SPENT A LOT OF TIME SITTING AROUND.

HERE. IF YOU'RE JUST MOPING ABOUT, YOU CAN HELP ME MIX THE PORRIDGE.

YOU CAN TELL YOU'RE BORED IF MIXING PORRIDGE SOUNDS LIKE A WELCOME DIVERSION.

FATUMA HAS LOTS OF RELATIVES WHO LIVE IN THE CAMP. THEY USUALLY COME BY DURING THE DAY WHEN I'M IN SCHOOL.

HELLO!

GALAB WANAAGSAN!

BUT I'M NOT IN SCHOOL TODAY.

AFTER THEY'RE DONE PINCHING AND PATTING...

HOW IS SCHOOL?

YOU'VE GOTTEN SO BIG!

...THEY SIT AND TALK FOR HOURS AND HOURS AND HOURS. STORIES ABOUT PEOPLE IN THE CAMP, OR STORIES AND POEMS FROM BEFORE.
FATUMA MOSTLY SITS AND LISTENS—SHE NEVER REALLY TALKS ABOUT HER LIFE BEFORE.
THEY ALSO TALK ABOUT NEWS THEY'VE HEARD FROM NEW ARRIVALS FROM SOMALIA. I SIT AND LISTEN TOO, HOPING FOR ANY SCRAP OF INFORMATION ABOUT MY MOTHER.
THE FIGHTING IS GETTING WORSE AND WORSE. IT'S BEEN NINE YEARS, AND STILL THE WAR IS RAGING ON!
I HEAR MORE PEOPLE ARE COMING TO DADAAB EVERY DAY.
SOON THERE WILL BE MORE SOMALIS HERE IN KENYA THAN THERE ARE IN SOMALIA!

A NEW GIRL— HAWA IS HER NAME. SHE JUST ARRIVED HERE LAST WEEK, FROM MAREEREY. SHE SAID THE WHOLE VILLAGE IS DESERTED— A GHOST TOWN. ALL THE FARMS ARE DESTROYED, CROPS BURNED TO THE GROUND. NOT A SOUL LEFT ALIVE, EXCEPT FOR THE ONES THE REBELS KIDNAPPED.

MAREEREY, WHY IS THAT NAME SO FAMILIAR...

OMAR! YOU'RE FROM MAREEREY, AREN'T YOU? THAT WAS YOUR VILLAGE?

LADAN! WHAT IS WRONG WITH YOU?!

I HAD TO GET OUT OF THERE.

HASSAN DIDN'T COMPLAIN, EVEN THOUGH WE WALKED AND WALKED UNTIL WE WERE ALMOST LOST IN THE BUSH. I KNEW IT WAS DANGEROUS OUT HERE, BUT I DIDN'T CARE. I FELT EMPTY AND NUMB INSIDE.

I FELT SO STUPID, LIKE A LITTLE KID PLAYING PRETEND ALL THESE YEARS. BUT NOW THE TRUTH WAS STARING ME IN THE FACE. I HAD TO STOP PRETENDING.

OUR VILLAGE WAS DESTROYED. WE COULD NEVER GO HOME AGAIN.

AND IF WE COULDN'T GO HOME, HOW COULD WE EVER...

WAS I ALSO PRETENDING...

NO. SHE WAS ALIVE. SHE **HAD** TO BE.

I LOVE MY MUM. BUT SOMETIMES I HATE HER FOR LEAVING US. IT'S LIKE THESE TWO FEELINGS ARE TEARING ME APART.

YOU SAID YOU WOULD COME FIND US. WELL, HERE WE ARE!

WE'RE HERE ALL ALONE! YOUR TWO SONS! DON'T YOU CARE?!?

DON'T YOU LOVE US?!

HASSAN AND I GET UP AND WALK BACK TO THE CAMP—ONE FOOT IN FRONT OF THE OTHER.

HER FRIENDS HAVE LEFT, BUT FATUMA IS STILL AWAKE, WAITING FOR US.

SHE MAY HAVE GOTTEN THE NAME WRONG. MAYBE IT WAS A DIFFERENT VILLAGE. MAYBE YOUR FARM IS STILL ALL RIGHT. EVERYTHING—

I KNOW, FATUMA. EVERYTHING WILL BE OK.

BUT I'M NOT A CHILD ANYMORE. I KNOW MAYBE EVERYTHING **WON'T** BE OK. BUT WE HAVE TO KEEP GOING ANYWAY, AND MAKE THE MOST WITH WHAT WE'VE GOT.

CHAPTER 7

I WAS SO HAPPY WHEN SCHOOL STARTED UP AGAIN.

‹WELCOME BACK, STUDENTS. TODAY WE WILL BEGIN PREPARING FOR YOUR END-OF-YEAR EXAMINATIONS.›

Exams

GULP.

...THEN AGAIN, MAYBE I SHOULD HAVE JUST STAYED HOME.

THAT DAY, EVERY SINGLE TEACHER TALKED ABOUT EXAMINATIONS. EVEN ARTS & CRAFTS— AND ALL WE DO IN THAT CLASS IS MAKE ELEPHANTS OUT OF MUD.

GEEZ, OUR TEACHERS ARE MAKING A REALLY BIG DEAL ABOUT THESE EXAMS, HUH?

WELL, THEY **ARE** A BIG DEAL. IF YOU DON'T PASS, YOU DON'T GO TO SCHOOL. THAT'S IT. **THE END**.

I KNEW THAT, OF COURSE. IN DADAAB, ANY KID CAN GO TO PRIMARY SCHOOL. IF THEIR FAMILIES LET THEM, THAT IS. BUT NOT EVERY KID CAN GO TO MIDDLE SCHOOL.

95

LOOK, THERE ARE A FEW PRIMARY SCHOOLS FOR DIFFERENT BLOCKS.

BUT THERE IS ONLY **ONE** MIDDLE SCHOOL— ALL THE WAY OVER HERE. SO ONLY THE BEST STUDENTS FROM EACH BLOCK GET TO GO TO MIDDLE SCHOOL.

HOW MANY KIDS FROM OUR CLASS WILL GET TO GO TO MIDDLE SCHOOL, DO YOU THINK?

I DON'T KNOW. MAYBE TEN STUDENTS? OR TWENTY? NO ONE REALLY KNOWS.

SO IF WE DON'T PASS— NO MORE SCHOOL.

IT'S STRANGE THAT JUST A FEW MONTHS AGO, I WASN'T EVEN SURE THAT I WANTED TO GO TO SCHOOL...

...AND NOW I WAS DESPERATE TO STAY.

IF I COULDN'T GO BACK TO MY VILLAGE...I GUESS I NEEDED SOMETHING TO BELIEVE IN. LIKE SCHOOL.

I HAVE TO KEEP GOING TO SCHOOL, JERI. I **HAVE** TO.

I CAN'T STAY AT HOME ALL DAY EITHER. I JUST... CAN'T.

I GUESS WE'D BETTER PASS THOSE TESTS, THEN.

TOGETHER.

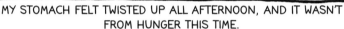

MY STOMACH FELT TWISTED UP ALL AFTERNOON, AND IT WASN'T FROM HUNGER THIS TIME.

<EXAM.>

<EXAM.>

<WE ONLY HAVE THREE MONTHS TO PREPARE FOR THIS EXAM, SO IF YOU HAVE NOTES, YOU'D BETTER START REVIEWING THEM.>

AT LEAST I HAD **ONE** ADVANTAGE. I WAS ONE OF THE FEW KIDS WHO HAD NOTES FROM CLASS.

NOT LIKE IT WOULD DO ME A TON OF GOOD. BY THE TIME I WALKED HOME...AND HAD ENGLISH CLASSES...AND PLAYED WITH HASSAN...AND CLEANED UP...AND DID ANY REPAIRS AROUND THE TENT...

RATS!

IT WAS COMPLETELY DARK, AND I HAD NO LIGHT.

C'MON! I'M **TRYING** TO STUDY AND WORK HARD! CAN'T I CATCH A BREAK?!

M...MUM?

I'VE GOT A LAMP, AND YOU'VE GOT THE NOTES. **TOGETHER**, RIGHT?

JERI AND I STARTED STUDYING TOGETHER EVERY NIGHT. SOON OTHER KIDS HEARD ABOUT OUR STUDY GROUP AND JOINED US— EVEN TALL ALI'S FRIENDS. TALL ALI KNEW BETTER THAN TO TRY AND JOIN US, THOUGH.

WE USUALLY MET IN MY TENT. I ONLY HAD HASSAN—MOST OF THE OTHER KIDS HAD A BUNCH OF YOUNGER SIBLINGS TO BOTHER US.

ONLY BOYS FROM MY CLASS CAME TO STUDY. NIMO AND MARYAM WOULD NEVER BE ALLOWED TO COME STUDY WITH A GROUP OF BOYS AT NIGHT.

I WONDER HOW THEY'RE DOING WITH THEIR STUDIES...

IT MIGHT SOUND WEIRD, BUT...I KIND OF **LIKED** STUDYING ALL THE TIME. IT FELT GOOD TO HAVE SOMETHING TO WORK TOWARD. A GOAL.

I GOT KIND OF OBSESSED. HASSAN WAS NOT HAPPY ABOUT IT.

HASSAN, **NO**. WE'RE STUDYING. LEAVE US ALONE.

HE DIDN'T LIKE THAT I STAYED AT SCHOOL LATER AND LATER, EVEN ON NIGHTS I DIDN'T HAVE ENGLISH LESSONS. I THINK HE WANTED ME TO BE ON HOLIDAY AGAIN, SO WE COULD PLAY TOGETHER ALL DAY.

HE CAN'T USE WORDS TO SAY HOW HE FEELS, AND I THINK THAT MAKES HIM FRUSTRATED.

FATUMA WAS HAVING A HARDER TIME KEEPING UP WITH HIM. HE RAN AWAY TWICE IN ONE WEEK, BUT NEIGHBOURS FOUND HIM AND BROUGHT HIM HOME.

FATUMA STARTED TYING THE DOOR SHUT WHEN SHE TOOK A NAP IN THE AFTERNOONS. I DON'T THINK HE LIKED BEING TRAPPED INDOORS **AT ALL**.

THE EXAMS WERE ALMOST HERE, THOUGH. WE ONLY HAD TO HOLD OUT FOR TWO MORE WEEKS. I COULD SEE SOME OF THE OTHER KIDS AT SCHOOL STARTING TO CRACK.

THERE WAS MUCH LESS LAUGHTER COMING FROM THE GIRLS' SIDE OF THE ROOM. YOU KNEW SOMETHING WAS WRONG IF NIMO WASN'T SINGING.

OUR STUDY GROUP WAS FEELING THE PRESSURE.

STOP CLICKING YOUR PEN! IT'S DRIVING ME CRAZY!

ONLY IF YOU STOP TAPPING YOUR LEG!

HASSAN! KNOCK IT OFF, WE'RE TRYING TO STUDY!

KICK

HASSAN, BUDDY? ARE YOU OK?

HE'LL BE FINE. LET'S KEEP STUDYING.

ONE WEEK LEFT.
OUR TEACHERS WERE GOING OVER LAST REVISIONS BEFORE OUR EXAMS. I NOTICED BOTH NIMO AND MARYAM WERE ABSENT—I WAS SURPRISED THEY WOULD MISS THIS.
<IMPORTANT DATES TO REMEMBER: IN 1962, THE KENYAN CONSTITUTION ESTABLISHED A BICAMERAL LEGISLATURE...>
AND THEN, JUST LIKE THAT—SCHOOL, EXAMS...NONE OF IT MATTERED ANYMORE.
OMAR! YOU NEED TO COME NOW! YOUR BROTHER HAS BEEN HURT!
SALAN! WHAT HAPPENED?
HASSAN BROKE OUT OF THE TENT WHILE FATUMA WAS SLEEPING, AND HE WANDERED OFF. SOME KIDS FOUND HIM IN A3 AND TOOK HIS CLOTHES, AND... WELL, HE'S PRETTY BADLY HURT.

SOME OF YOUR NEIGHBOURS FOUND HIM AND BROUGHT HIM HOME AND...

SLOW DOWN!

HE'S WEARING NEW CLOTHES—ONE OF THE NEIGHBOURS MUST HAVE GIVEN THEM TO HIM.

NO BROKEN BONES, NO MAJOR INJURIES. IT COULD HAVE BEEN MUCH WORSE.

IT COULD HAVE BEEN WORSE. BUT IT **WON'T** BE. NOTHING LIKE THIS WILL EVER HAPPEN AGAIN.

I'M HERE NOW. I'M NOT LEAVING. DON'T WORRY. EVERYTHING WILL BE OK.

JERI CAME BY AFTER SCHOOL WITH MY NOTEBOOK, BUT I TOLD HIM TO KEEP IT. I'VE BEEN SELFISH LONG ENOUGH. OBVIOUSLY I WAS WRONG ABOUT SCHOOL—I NEED TO BE WITH MY BROTHER.

THE NEXT DAY, I DIDN'T LEAVE HASSAN'S SIDE. I WAS HIS ONLY FAMILY—HOW COULD I HAVE FORGOTTEN THAT IT WAS MY JOB TO TAKE CARE OF HIM?

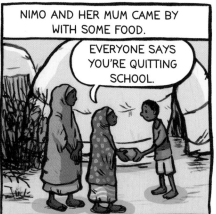

NIMO AND HER MUM CAME BY WITH SOME FOOD.

EVERYONE SAYS YOU'RE QUITTING SCHOOL.

I NEED TO STAY HERE WITH HASSAN.

BUT HEY, THAT'S GOOD NEWS FOR YOU AND MARYAM, RIGHT? ONE LESS PERSON TO COMPETE WITH FOR CANADA?

WHAT...WHAT DID I SAY?

SIGH IT'S NOT YOU. IT'S MARYAM.

HER FATHER HAS ARRANGED FOR HER TO BE MARRIED NEXT MONTH. HE'S NOT LETTING HER TAKE THE EXAMS. HE SAYS THERE'S NO POINT SINCE SHE WON'T BE CONTINUING ON IN SCHOOL.

BUT...BUT MARYAM'S BEEN STUDYING SO HARD! AND EXAMS ARE NEXT WEEK! THAT'S SO UNFAIR!
OMAR, I'VE LEARNED NOT TO JUDGE OTHERS TOO HARSHLY. FAMILIES HERE ARE DESPERATE. MARYAM HAS THREE YOUNGER SIBLINGS, AND HER PARENTS NEED TO THINK ABOUT ALL OF THEM.
HER FATHER FOUND A KIND MAN FOR MARYAM, AND THE MONEY FROM THE UNION WILL HELP THE FAMILY.
BUT YOU SEND **NIMO** TO SCHOOL! YOU SAY IT'S IMPORTANT FOR GIRLS TO HAVE AN EDUCATION!
I AM LUCKY. I HAVE TWO SONS WHO PROVIDE FOR ME, AND I CAN SELL MY BASKETS FOR GOOD MONEY. I CAN AFFORD TO SEND MY DAUGHTER TO SCHOOL.
THERE ARE MANY PEOPLE IN THIS WORLD LESS FORTUNATE THAN YOU AND I. REMEMBER THAT, OMAR.
I HAD A HARD TIME BELIEVING THAT I OR ANYONE IN THIS CAMP WAS **FORTUNATE**. LIFE HERE WAS JUST SO UNFAIR.

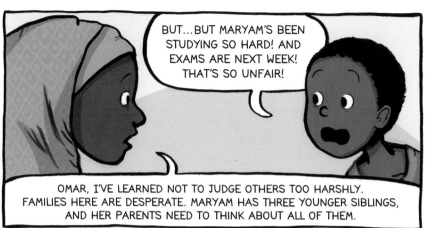

HASSAN STARTED TO GET BETTER, AND SOON IT'S THE DAY BEFORE EXAMS. I CAN'T HELP BUT THINK ABOUT ALL MY CLASSMATES PREPARING FOR THE TESTS. I WONDER WHO WILL PASS AND WHO WILL FAIL. I WONDER HOW MARYAM WOULD HAVE DONE. I WONDER HOW **I** WOULD HAVE DONE.

MAYBE I CAN GO BACK TO SCHOOL. SOMEDAY.

HEY.

OH. HI, MARYAM.

I HEARD YOU'RE QUITTING SCHOOL.

YEAH. I HAVE TO TAKE CARE OF HASSAN. **YOU** OF ALL PEOPLE MUST UNDERSTAND.

NO, I **DON'T** UNDERSTAND. I DON'T UNDERSTAND HOW **ANYONE** WOULD TURN DOWN THE CHANCE TO GO TO SCHOOL.

DO YOU THINK IF I WERE A **BOY** I'D BE FORCED TO QUIT SCHOOL? NO. I COULD HAVE GONE TO CANADA. I **KNOW** I COULD HAVE DONE IT, AND BROUGHT MY WHOLE FAMILY WITH ME. NOW I DON'T HAVE A CHANCE.

NOW I HAVE TO MARRY SOMEONE I DON'T EVEN KNOW, AND I'M **TERRIFIED**. DO YOU UNDERSTAND ME? I'M **TERRIFIED**.

MY DREAMS, MY HOPES FOR MY FAMILY—THEY'RE **OVER**. AND YOU'RE JUST THROWING YOUR CHANCE AWAY.

BUT HASSAN...

YOU'RE USING HASSAN AS AN **EXCUSE**. YOU THINK YOU'RE HELPING HIM BY ALWAYS HOVERING OVER HIM AND TRYING TO FIGHT ALL HIS BATTLES FOR HIM. BUT HE'S MORE CAPABLE THAN YOU THINK HE IS.

HE...HE GOT BEAT UP! I WASN'T HERE TO PROTECT HIM!

EVERYONE IN A2 WOULD PROTECT HASSAN IF HE WERE IN TROUBLE. WHO BROUGHT HIM HOME, AFTER ALL? YOU'RE NOT THE ONLY ONE WHO CARES FOR HIM, YOU KNOW.

YOU HAVE A GIFT, OMAR. YOU'RE SMART, AND YOU'RE KIND. YOU COULD HELP HASSAN AND OTHER REFUGEES LIKE HIM—OTHER REFUGEES LIKE **ME**—IF YOU KEEP GOING TO SCHOOL.

I THINK YOU'RE BEING **SELFISH**.

STOP CRYING, ANISA. WE HAVE TO GO HOME AND MAKE TEA.

SELFISH!

MUM TOLD ME TO TAKE CARE OF YOU, AND THAT'S WHAT I'M **DOING**! HOW DARE SHE CALL ME **SELFISH**?!

I KNOW. HOOYO.

I DIDN'T TELL HASSAN ANY STORIES THAT NIGHT. INSTEAD, I SPEND THE WHOLE NIGHT ARGUING WITH MYSELF.

I COULDN'T TAKE THE EXAMS TOMORROW ANYWAY, EVEN IF I WANTED TO! I HAVEN'T STUDIED IN A WEEK! AND HOW AM I BEING SELFISH WHEN I'M JUST TAKING CARE OF MY FAMILY?

WHEN HASSAN FINALLY FELL ASLEEP, I WENT OUTSIDE TO THINK. MAYBE OUTSIDE, I'D UNDERSTAND WHAT MY PARENTS WOULD WANT ME TO DO.

BUT INSTEAD OF MY PARENTS, I FOUND...

FATUMA? WHAT ARE YOU DOING AWAKE?

I'M SORRY HASSAN RAN AWAY, OMAR. I'M AN OLD WOMAN, AND I CAN'T KEEP UP WITH YOUR BROTHER LIKE I'D WANT TO.

MARYAM SAYS I'M BEING OVER-PROTECTIVE. SHE SAYS THERE ARE LOTS OF PEOPLE WHO LOVE HASSAN, THAT I CAN'T WATCH OVER HIM ALL THE TIME.

WELL, THAT'S TRUE. THAT IS A GIFT THAT GOD HAS GIVEN HIM. HASSAN IS CONSIDERATE, HELPFUL AND FRIENDLY, AND HE IS LOVED BY MANY.

I NEVER THOUGHT BEING FRIENDLY WAS A **GIFT**. I THOUGHT...IT'S JUST THE WAY HE **IS**. MAYBE I WAS WRONG.

EVERY HUMAN IS A GIFT, JUST THE WAY GOD MAKES US. AND **LOVE** IS A GIFT. GOD HAS GIVEN YOU THE GIFT OF A COMMUNITY OF PEOPLE WHO WILL LOVE AND PROTECT YOU AND YOUR BROTHER. YOU SHOULD PRAY TO GOD AND THANK HIM. HE WILL SHOW YOU WHAT TO DO NEXT.

I DON'T KNOW IF IT'S TECHNICALLY PRAYING... BUT I DRIFT OFF TO SLEEP STARING AT MY BROTHER, AND I THANK GOD FOR ALL THE **GOOD** THINGS WE HAVE.

THEN IT IS THE NEXT MORNING. EXAM DAY.

I SAY MY MORNING PRAYERS.

I WAKE UP HASSAN. WE GO TO FATUMA'S TENT.

MARYAM IS THERE.

I AM WATCHING HASSAN TODAY. I WILL CHANGE HIS BANDAGES, AND I WILL WATCH HIM ALONG WITH MY OWN BROTHERS AND SISTER. **YOU** WILL GO TAKE YOUR EXAMS.

BUT...

BUT **WHAT?**

BUT...BUT...I HAVEN'T STUDIED IN A **WEEK**! MAYBE I'LL FAIL!

MAYBE YOU **WILL** FAIL, AND YOU WON'T HAVE TO GO TO SCHOOL ANYMORE. MAYBE YOU'LL **PASS**, AND YOU'LL HAVE TO FIGURE OUT YOUR NEXT STEPS THEN. THERE'S ONLY ONE WAY TO FIND OUT.

I...I...

I AM GIVING YOU A CHANCE, OMAR. A CHANCE I DON'T HAVE. ARE YOU GOING TO TAKE IT, OR NOT?

I KNOW MY DECISION.

THANK YOU, MARYAM.

NOW I UNDERSTAND WHAT NIMO'S MUM AND FATUMA WERE TELLING ME. I **AM** LUCKY. SO MANY PEOPLE LOVE AND SUPPORT ME AND HASSAN. FATUMA, SALAN, MARYAM, JERI, ALL OF OUR NEIGHBOURS. I CAN HAVE FAITH IN MY COMMUNITY.

I'LL BE BACK SOON. HELP MARYAM AND FATUMA, OK?

WE MAY BE REFUGEES AND ORPHANS, BUT WE ARE NOT ALONE. GOD HAS GIVEN US THE GIFT OF LOVE.

AND LIKE SALAN TOLD ME, BACK WHEN I FIRST STARTED SCHOOL...

...WHEN GOD GIVES YOU A GIFT, IT IS YOUR JOB TO USE IT.

DANTEY!

I KNEW YOU WOULD COME!

YOU THINK YOU CAN JUST SHOW UP ON EXAM DAY AND PASS? GOOD LUCK WITH THAT.

I'VE GOT ALL THE LUCK I NEED, ALI. I WISH THE SAME GOOD LUCK TO YOU.

GOOD LUCK, NIMO.

I DON'T NEED LUCK EITHER. I WILL PASS MY EXAMS.

I'LL PASS THEM FOR MARYAM.

I'D NEVER SEEN MY CLASSMATES SO NERVOUS. THEY EITHER WEREN'T TALKING AT ALL...OR TALKING **TOO** MUCH AND **TOO** LOUD.

EVEN FOR CLASSMATES I **DIDN'T** LIKE...IT DIDN'T SEEM FAIR. WE WERE ALL JUST KIDS WHO WANTED TO GO TO SCHOOL.

AT LEAST IN EXAMS—UNLIKE REAL LIFE—THERE WOULD BE RIGHT AND WRONG ANSWERS.

PASS OR FAIL—I'VE DONE MY BEST. IT'S IN GOD'S HANDS NOW.

I TAKE A DEEP BREATH.

Name: Omar Mohamed

Question 1:

PART 2

TWO YEARS LATER

IN A REFUGEE CAMP, EVERYTHING CAN CHANGE...AND NOTHING CAN CHANGE.
I'M STILL HERE. SO **THAT** HASN'T CHANGED.

BUT...WE HAVE A GOAT! ONE OF FATUMA'S FRIENDS GAVE IT TO HER WHEN SHE GOT RESETTLED TO SWEDEN.

HEY! QUIT BITING MY SHIRT!

BROWNIE HATES ME AND IS MY SWORN ENEMY...BUT NOW WE HAVE MILK TO DRINK AND WE CAN SELL THE EXTRA MILK. THAT MEANS WE CAN SOMETIMES BUY THINGS LIKE SHOES AND CLOTHES. I THINK THAT'S WHY BROWNIE TORTURES ME SO—SHE KNOWS I CAN'T GET RID OF HER.

YOU MAY HAVE ALSO NOTICED MY SWANKY NEW OUTFIT. ONE OF FATUMA'S FRIEND'S SON DIED, AND HE WAS ABOUT MY SIZE. HE HAD DIABETES. I DIDN'T KNOW HIM, OTHERWISE IT MIGHT HAVE BEEN WEIRD WEARING A DEAD KID'S CLOTHES. ACTUALLY, IT'S STILL A LITTLE WEIRD WHEN I THINK ABOUT IT.

HIS HEART WAS BEATING RIGHT HERE, WHERE MY HEART IS.

SOMETIMES I SAY A LITTLE THANK-YOU TO HIM WHEN I PUT MY CLOTHES ON IN THE MORNING.

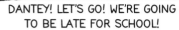
DANTEY! LET'S GO! WE'RE GOING TO BE LATE FOR SCHOOL!

THAT'S RIGHT, I'M IN MIDDLE SCHOOL! I PASSED THE EXAMS!

HASSAN? I'M LEAVING NOW. I'LL BE BACK THIS AFTERNOON.

...HASSAN?

I GUESS I DIDN'T HAVE TO WORRY SO MUCH ABOUT LEAVING HIM ALONE. HE BARELY NOTICES I'M GONE BECAUSE HE'S SO BUSY TAKING CARE OF BROWNIE. HE GIVES HER FRESH WATER EVERY MORNING, AND THEN HE AND FATUMA TAKE HER ON LONG WALKS TO LET HER GRAZE. HASSAN IS REALLY GOOD WITH ANIMALS. I THINK HE WOULD MAKE A MUCH BETTER FARMER THAN ME.

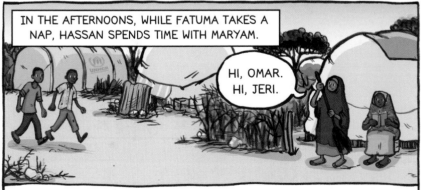
IN THE AFTERNOONS, WHILE FATUMA TAKES A NAP, HASSAN SPENDS TIME WITH MARYAM.

HI, OMAR. HI, JERI.

MARYAM'S HUSBAND IS OLD, BUT HE'S NOT TOO STRICT. HE DOESN'T MIND THAT SHE SPENDS TIME WITH HASSAN IN THE AFTERNOON OR THAT SHE STILL STUDIES WITH NIMO—SO LONG AS HER CHORES GET DONE.

COME ON, NIMO! WE'RE GOING TO BE LATE!

I'LL COME BY AFTER SCHOOL.

DON'T FORGET TO ASK YOUR TEACHER THAT QUESTION I HAD ABOUT PHOTOSYNTHESIS, OK?

NIMO PASSED HER EXAMS TOO—**OF COURSE**. SHE EVEN GOT THE TOP SCORE FOR GIRLS. BUT WHO KNOWS WHAT WOULD HAVE HAPPENED IF...

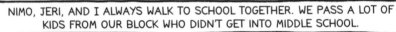

NIMO, JERI, AND I ALWAYS WALK TO SCHOOL TOGETHER. WE PASS A LOT OF KIDS FROM OUR BLOCK WHO DIDN'T GET INTO MIDDLE SCHOOL.

HEY! YOU GUYS! FOOTBALL LATER?

YEAH, IF WE DON'T HAVE TOO MUCH HOMEWORK. SURE!

I FEEL BAD FOR TALL ALI, EVEN IF HE IS A JERK. I REMEMBER HOW IT FELT TO STAY HOME WHILE MY FRIENDS WENT TO SCHOOL.

OUR MIDDLE SCHOOL LOOKS A LOT LIKE OUR PRIMARY SCHOOL, BUT IT'S NOT AS CROWDED.

WE HAVE THIRTY-SEVEN BOYS AND TWELVE GIRLS IN OUR CLASS.

WE START EACH DAY OFF WITH ASSEMBLY. THE WHOLE SCHOOL SITS OUTSIDE, AND WE POUR WATER ON THE GROUND SO WE DON'T GET ALL DUSTY. ASSEMBLY IS USUALLY PRETTY BORING— TEACHERS TELL US ABOUT SCHOOL SCHEDULES, OR CLUB MEETINGS, OR UPCOMING EXAMS. BUT ASSEMBLY IS GREAT WHEN...

YES! IT'S MICHAEL!

MICHAEL IS OUR ENGLISH TEACHER. I THINK BACK IN SOMALIA HE WOULD HAVE BEEN ONE OF THOSE POETS NIMO'S MUM ALWAYS TALKS ABOUT.

<GOOD MORNING!>

HE HAS A WAY OF USING HIS WORDS TO TAKE YOU TO A DIFFERENT PLACE.

<STUDENTS, I'D LIKE YOU TO CLOSE YOUR EYES...AND IMAGINE THE NIGHT SKY.>

<NOW IMAGINE YOURSELF AS ONE OF THOSE STARS. YOUR LIGHT IS BRIGHT AND SHINES FOR MILLIONS OF MILES.>

<NOW OPEN YOUR EYES, AND OPEN THEM WIDE. LOOK AT YOUR FRIENDS SITTING ALL AROUND YOU.>

<THROUGHOUT YOUR LIFE, PEOPLE MAY SHOUT UGLY WORDS AT YOU. WORDS LIKE, "GO HOME, REFUGEE!" OR "YOU HAVE NO RIGHT TO BE HERE!">

<WHEN YOU MEET THESE PEOPLE, TELL THEM TO LOOK AT THE STARS, AND HOW THEY MOVE ACROSS THE SKY. NO ONE TELLS A STAR TO GO HOME.>

<TELL THEM, "I AM A STAR. I DESERVE TO EXIST JUST THE SAME AS A STAR. HOW DO I KNOW?>

<"BECAUSE HERE I AM. I AM HERE. THE PROOF IS IN THE STARS.">

COMING FROM SOMEONE ELSE, THIS SPEECH MIGHT SOUND CHEESY. BUT MICHAEL HAS A WAY OF MAKING YOU BELIEVE IN YOURSELF.

THEN IT'S INSIDE FOR CLASSES. ENGLISH IS FIRST.

TODAY WE'RE READING ESSAYS WE WROTE (IN ENGLISH, OF COURSE) ABOUT WHAT WE WANT TO BE WHEN WE GROW UP.

<OMAR, YOU'RE UP!>

<WHEN I GROW UP, I WANT TO BE A SOCIAL WORKER WITH THE UNITED NATIONS. SOCIAL WORKERS ARE NICE. THEY ARE HELPFUL. THEY HELP PEOPLE GET FOOD WHEN THEY ARE HUNGRY. THEY HELP YOU SEE A DOCTOR IF YOU ARE SICK. THAT IS WHY I WANT TO BE A SOCIAL WORKER.>

I STILL HAVE DREAMS ABOUT OUR FARM IN SOMALIA. BUT I'M TRYING TO FORGET. YOU CAN'T LIVE IN THE PAST, AND DREAMS AREN'T REAL.

<VERY NICE, OMAR. YOU MAY TAKE YOUR SEAT.>

BESIDES, I THINK I'D BE A GOOD SOCIAL WORKER. MAYBE I CAN HELP MAKE THINGS MORE FAIR FOR REFUGEES WHO CAN'T STAND UP FOR THEMSELVES.

<NEXT IS...NIMO! COME ON UP, NIMO.>

AHEM <WHEN I GROW UP, I'D LIKE TO BE A LAWYER. LAWYERS HAVE TO ARGUE CASES IN COURT, AND I THINK I'D BE GOOD AT THAT.>

I'LL SAY SHE'D BE GOOD AT THAT!

<LAWYERS CAN HELP PEOPLE KNOW THEIR RIGHTS. I WANT TO HELP WOMEN AND GIRL REFUGEES KNOW THEIR RIGHTS. I WANT TO MAKE LIFE FAIR FOR THEM.>

<A VERY WORTHY GOAL, NIMO. THANK YOU.>

NIMO HASN'T TALKED MUCH ABOUT BECOMING AN ACTRESS OR A SINGER RECENTLY. IN FACT, SHE'S BEEN A LOT QUIETER, FULL STOP. I HAVEN'T HEARD HER SING FOR THE LONGEST TIME.

THE OTHER STUDENTS HAD YOUR STANDARD ANSWERS FOR WHAT THEY WANTED TO BE WHEN THEY GREW UP. FOOTBALL PLAYER, PILOT, PRESIDENT OF KENYA, PRESIDENT OF SOMALIA.

<JERI, MY BOY! YOU'RE UP!>

I SAT UP STRAIGHT. I WAS CURIOUS WHAT JERI HAD WRITTEN ABOUT. WHEN WE TALK ABOUT THE FUTURE, HE MOSTLY TALKS ABOUT GOING TO AMERICA.

I COULD TELL JERI WAS NERVOUS BY THE WAY HE WAS TAPPING HIS LEG.

<WHEN I GROW UP, I'D LIKE TO BE...A TEACHER. MAYBE AN ENGLISH TEACHER. TEACHERS CAN INSPIRE THEIR STUDENTS. THEY CAN GIVE THEIR STUDENTS HOPE FOR THEIR FUTURE, AND MAKE THEM BELIEVE THEY CAN DO ANYTHING THEY WANT. I THINK IT IS A VERY NICE THING TO BE A TEACHER.>

<IT IS INDEED A VERY NICE THING TO BE A TEACHER. AND YOU WILL BE AN EXCELLENT ONE. I CAN JUST TELL THAT ABOUT YOU. YOU MAY TAKE YOUR SEAT.>

WHAT A SUCK-UP.

A TEACHER. HUH. I TRIED TO CATCH JERI'S EYE, BUT HE JUST STARED AT HIS PENCIL FOR THE REST OF THE CLASS.

AFTER SCHOOL, WE WALKED HOME TOGETHER, AS USUAL.

HEY, JERI! I DIDN'T KNOW YOU WANTED TO BE A TEACHER!

GO AHEAD AND LAUGH.

I'M NOT LAUGHING! I THINK YOU'D BE A GOOD TEACHER!

YEAH, RIGHT.

OW!

OH! UM, YOU WOULD BE A GOOD TEACHER. YOU ALWAYS HELPED ME WHEN WE WERE STUDYING FOR EXAMS. I GOT INTO MIDDLE SCHOOL, DIDN'T I?

AND YOU WERE NUMBER THIRTY-THREE WHEN WE STARTED. I HAD VERY LITTLE TO WORK WITH.

HEY! YOU TOLD ME THIRTY-THREE WASN'T SO BAD!

OUR NEW WALK HOME TOOK US RIGHT BY THE MARKET. USUALLY WE KEEP ON WALKING, BUT TODAY...

HEY, CAN WE STOP FOR A MINUTE? MY MUM WANTED ME TO BUY SOME SUGAR.

UM, I'M SUPPOSED TO GO STRAIGHT HOME...

PLEEEEEEASE? YOU KNOW I DON'T LIKE TO WALK THROUGH THE MARKET BY MYSELF. COME ON, IT WILL ONLY TAKE A MINUTE.

HRMMPH.

WHAT'S WITH HIM?

SHRUG

OF COURSE, NIMO STARTED CHATTING WITH THE SUGAR SELLER...

AND WITH THE CLOTHING SELLER...

AND A NEIGHBOUR WE MET ON THE STREET...

NOW CAN WE GET OUT OF HERE? PLEASE?

IS THAT MY SON I HEAR? GET OVER HERE, LIMPY!

GREAT. THANKS A LOT.

HEY, LOOK EVERYONE! IT'S MY SON! WE CALL HIM LIMPY! HE COULD BARELY WALK WHEN HE WAS SMALLER.

JERI'S DAD LOOKED A LOT DIFFERENT THAN THE LAST TIME I SAW HIM. HIS EYES WERE ALL RED, AND HIS FACE LOOKED SUNKEN IN. HE AND THE MEN SITTING AROUND HIM WERE ALL CHEWING KHAT LEAVES. A LOT OF THE MEN IN CAMP CHEW KHAT. THEY SAY IT KIND OF HELPS YOU...FORGET THINGS.

I CAN WALK NOW, DAD.

HEY! WHERE WERE YOU TODAY? WERE YOU IN SCHOOL? ARE YOU STILL IN SCHOOL? WHAT DO THEY TEACH YOU AT THAT SCHOOL OF YOURS? WHAT DID YOU DO TODAY?

WE, UM...

SPEAK UP! I CAN'T HEAR YOU!

WE READ ESSAYS WE WROTE. ABOUT WHAT WE WANT TO BE WHEN WE GROW UP.

HA! GOOD ONE! I CAN TELL YOU WHAT YOU'LL BE—YOU'LL BE A REFUGEE.

AND WHAT DID YOU SAY? WHAT DO YOU WANT TO BE WHEN YOU GROW UP?

I THINK...I MAYBE WANT TO BE...A TEACHER?

YEAH RIGHT. I DON'T THINK PEOPLE LIKE **YOU** CAN BE TEACHERS, **LIMPY**.

AND YOU, WHAT DO **YOU** WANT TO BE?

ME, SIR? I...UH, WANT TO WORK FOR THE UN...

OH BOY, HERE HE GOES...

THE **UN**? THE **UN**! DON'T TALK TO ME ABOUT THE UN! WORTHLESS CROOKS! IT'S THEIR JOB TO HELP REFUGEES! DO THEY HELP ME? DO THEY LISTEN WHEN I SAY MY LIFE IS IN DANGER IN SOMALIA AND I HAVE TO BE RESETTLED? NO! THEY HELP NOBODY BUT THEMSELVES, WITH THEIR FANCY CARS AND THEIR BIG COMPOUNDS.

THIS IS WHAT THEY TEACH YOU IN SCHOOLS? FILL YOUR HEADS WITH CRAZY DREAMS ABOUT WHAT YOU CAN BE? TEACH **GIRLS** AND TELL THEM THEY CAN BE ANYTHING THEY WANT?

NIMO KIND OF HID BEHIND US AND KEPT HER HEAD DOWN.

AND **YOU**, MY OWN SON, YOU WANT TO BE A **TEACHER**? HOW WILL YOU GET A JOB? REFUGEES AREN'T ALLOWED TO WORK!

MY TEACHER, MICHAEL... HE'S A REFUGEE...

THEN THEY PROBABLY PAY HIM **ONE-TENTH** OF WHAT THEY'D PAY A KENYAN FOR THE SAME WORK. US REFUGEES, WE ARE NOTHING BUT SLAVE LABOUR AROUND HERE. LOOK AROUND YOU. WE'RE SURROUNDED BY DESERT. YOU'RE IN A **PRISON** RIGHT NOW. A GIANT, SPRAWLING PRISON—AND YOU'LL SPEND THE REST OF YOUR LIFE HERE. AND THAT'S THE **REAL** TRUTH YOUR TEACHERS WON'T TELL YOU ABOUT.

NOW GET OUT OF HERE. GET OUT OF MY FACE.

WELL, THAT WAS UPLIFTING.

SHUT UP.

OUR WALK HOME WAS PRETTY QUIET AFTER THAT.

HELLO? I'M HOME.

EVER SINCE BROWNIE ENTERED OUR LIVES, NO WARM WELCOMES FOR ME.

OH! OMAR! YOU'RE BACK.

FATUMA...IS IT STUPID OF ME TO BE GOING TO SCHOOL? WHAT'S THE POINT OF GOING TO SCHOOL IF I CAN'T GET A JOB AFTERWARD?

WELL...WE NEVER KNOW WHAT WILL HAPPEN IN OUR LIVES, DO WE? GOD SURPRISES US, AND PROVIDES WHEN HE WILL. LIKE WHEN HE BROUGHT US BROWNIE!

EVERYTHING COMES BACK TO THAT STUPID GOAT.

SO STAY IN SCHOOL. PREPARE YOURSELF AND EDUCATE YOURSELF, SO YOU CAN BE READY WHEN GOD REVEALS HIS PLAN TO YOU.

IT'S LIKE A PRISON HERE.

YOU'RE ALIVE, AREN'T YOU? YOU'RE GOING TO SCHOOL? LIFE IS ONLY A PRISON IF YOU MAKE IT ONE. THINK OF THIS MORE LIKE...GOD'S WAITING ROOM.

THAT'S WHAT THIS REFUGEE CAMP FELT LIKE. A GIANT WAITING ROOM, FILLED WITH HUNDREDS OF THOUSANDS OF PEOPLE. WAITING AND WAITING AND WAITING.

EVERYONE HERE JUST WANTS A PLACE TO CALL HOME. A PLACE WHERE THEY CAN WORK, OR GO TO SCHOOL. A PLACE WHERE THEIR FAMILIES WILL BE SAFE.

BUT HOW CAN YOU HAVE A HOME WHEN YOU LIVE IN A WAITING ROOM? MAYBE JERI'S DAD IS RIGHT, BECAUSE SOMETIMES IT SURE FEELS LIKE A PRISON TO ME.

CHAPTER 8

WALKING TO SCHOOL THE NEXT DAY, I COULD TELL JERI HAD BEEN THINKING ABOUT WHAT HIS DAD HAD SAID TOO. IT'S LIKE OVERNIGHT WE SUDDENLY BECAME GROWN-UPS AND HAD TO DECIDE OUR FUTURES, RIGHT NOW.

I HEAR SOME PEOPLE SNEAK OFF TO NAIROBI AND FIND JOBS THERE. MAYBE THAT'S WHAT I'LL DO.

ISN'T THAT... **ILLEGAL**? WE CAN'T WORK IN NAIROBI BECAUSE WE'RE NOT KENYAN.

SO? WE CAN'T WORK HERE, EITHER. WHAT'S THE DIFFERENCE?

MY BROTHERS ARE INTERPRETERS. **THEY** HAVE JOBS.

YEAH RIGHT. SOME JOB. IT'S JUST LIKE BEING A TEACHER— IT'S NOT A **REAL** JOB. REFUGEES AREN'T ALLOWED TO HAVE REAL JOBS. SO WE WORK FOR SCRAPS. WE SELL FIREWOOD OR UNLOAD CARTS IN THE MARKET FOR **SCRAPS**. WE LIVE OFF OF **SCRAPS** UNTIL WE **DIE**.

I KNOW I LIKE TO BE LEFT ALONE WHEN I'M IN ONE OF THOSE MOODS, SO I JUST KEPT MY MOUTH SHUT.

HEY, YOU GUYS! WAIT UP! YOU'RE NEVER GOING TO BELIEVE IT! REMEMBER ABDIKARIM?

THAT KID WE USED TO PLAY FOOTBALL WITH?

YEAH— WHAT ABOUT HIM?

HE'S GETTING RESETTLED! TO **AMERICA**! COME ON, EVERYONE IS AT HIS TENT!

A BIG CROWD HAD GATHERED BY THE TIME WE GOT TO ABDIKARIM'S TENT.

IT'S JUST OUR FIRST INTERVIEW WITH THE UN! THERE'S NO TELLING IF WE'LL ACTUALLY GO.

HOW WONDERFUL!

CONGRATULATIONS!

I WOULDN'T WANT TO GO TO AMERICA. NO MORALS THERE.

OH, YOU'RE JUST JEALOUS. YOU KNOW YOU'D GO IN A HEARTBEAT IF YOU COULD!

DID YOU HEAR? WE'RE GOING TO AMERICA!

WHEN ARE YOU GOING?

HOW DID YOU FIND OUT?

YOU'RE GOING TO BE RICH!

UGH, WHAT'S THE POINT OF HANGING AROUND HERE? WE'VE GOT TO GO, OR WE'LL BE LATE FOR SCHOOL!

WHAT'S THE **POINT**? ARE YOU **CRAZY**? **HE'S GOING TO AMERICA!** MAYBE WE'LL FIND OUT HOW HE DID IT!

YOU'RE WASTING YOUR TIME DREAMING ABOUT IT. DON'T YOU KNOW THE CHANCES OF GETTING RESETTLED ARE ABOUT A MILLION TO ONE?

WELL? OMAR? ARE YOU COMING, OR ARE YOU STAYING?

WELL...MAYBE WE **CAN** LEARN HOW HE DID IT...

RRRGGGH! YOU'RE WASTING YOUR TIME, ALL OF YOU!

WILL YOU GET A BIG HOUSE?

OF COURSE HE'LL GET A BIG HOUSE! EVERYONE IN AMERICA HAS A BIG HOUSE!

AND A FANCY CAR!

WHERE ARE YOU GOING? NEW YORK? OR CALIFORNIA?

SO? HOW DID YOUR DAD DO IT? HOW DID YOUR FAMILY GET PICKED?

I DUNNO, OUR NAME WAS JUST ON THE LIST.

THE LIST. EVERYONE IN DADAAB KNOWS ABOUT THE LIST.

EVERY WEEK, THE UN POSTS A LIST OF PEOPLE TO COME IN TO INTERVIEW FOR RESETTLEMENT. EVERYONE SAYS THE WAY TO GET ON THE LIST IS TO SAY YOUR LIFE IS IN DANGER. LIKE, YOU'RE FROM A MINORITY CLAN OR RELIGION, OR YOUR LIFE WAS THREATENED BACK IN SOMALIA.

I GUESS BEING AN ORPHAN AND HASSAN'S DISABILITIES AREN'T ENOUGH OF A DANGER, BECAUSE IT'S BEEN NINE YEARS AND OUR NAMES HAVE NEVER BEEN ON THE LIST.

JERI AND I STAYED AND TALKED WITH THE OTHER BOYS ABOUT AMERICA, AND WHAT IT WOULD BE LIKE TO LIVE THERE. BEFORE WE KNEW IT...

HEY! IT'S GETTING DARK. WE MISSED THE WHOLE DAY OF SCHOOL. WE'D BETTER GO HOME.

AMERICA.

YEAH.

I...I THOUGHT YOUR DAD PAID SOME MONEY TO GET YOUR CASE HEARD...

YEAH? AND YOU SEE HOW WELL THAT WORKED. NOW HE'S JUST BROKE. AND HE DOESN'T EVEN WORK AT THE MARKET ANYMORE. HE JUST SITS AROUND WITH HIS FRIENDS CHEWING KHAT.

I HOPE MY DAD HASN'T HEARD ABOUT ABDIKARIM'S FAMILY GETTING RESETTLED, HE'LL BE REALLY ANGRY...

135

DO YOU WANT TO SLEEP OVER?

NO, I'D BETTER GO BACK HOME. MY MUM AND MY BROTHERS AND SISTERS ARE THERE. I'LL SEE YOU TOMORROW.

I DIDN'T TALK MUCH THAT EVENING. I ONLY HAD ONE THING ON MY MIND ALL NIGHT...

AMERICA.

I NEVER REALLY THOUGHT ABOUT GOING TO AMERICA BEFORE. NOT FOR REAL. IT SEEMED IMPOSSIBLE. THE CHANCES WERE A MILLION TO ONE.

BUT NOW, SOMEONE I KNEW WAS GOING.

UNROLL

ABDIKARIM HAD FOUND A WAY OUT OF THIS PRISON WE WERE ALL STUCK IN.

I DIDN'T KNOW MUCH ABOUT AMERICA. SOME PEOPLE SAID THAT LIFE THERE IS NOT EASY, THAT PEOPLE LOOKED DOWN ON REFUGEES. BUT SURELY LIFE IN AMERICA HAD TO BE BETTER THAN **THIS**?

I KNEW YOU COULD AT LEAST GO TO **SCHOOL** IN AMERICA. YOU COULD GET A **JOB**.

MAYBE IN AMERICA, WE COULD BE SAFE. WE COULD HAVE A HOME.

ALL THESE THOUGHTS AND MORE SETTLE ON ME LIKE A HEAVY WEIGHT.

I BET SOME OTHER KID IN AMERICA IS ASLEEP RIGHT NOW IN THEIR CLEAN, SOFT, COMFORTABLE BED, WHILE I'M SLEEPING IN THE **DIRT**.

WHY DOES ABDIKARIM GET TO LEAVE, AND I HAVE TO STAY HERE?

WHY DO SOME KIDS HAVE EVERYTHING, AND I HAVE **NOTHING**?

IT'S NOT FAIR.

OF COURSE, THINKING LIKE THIS DOESN'T DO YOU ANY GOOD. SOMALIS EVEN HAVE A WORD FOR IT. **BUUFIS.** IT MEANS THE INTENSE LONGING TO BE RESETTLED. IT'S ALMOST LIKE YOUR MIND IS ALREADY LIVING SOMEWHERE ELSE, WHILE YOUR BODY IS STUCK IN A REFUGEE CAMP.

IT'S NOT FAIR.

IT'S NOT FAIR.

IT'S NOT FAIR.

IT DRIVES SOME PEOPLE INSANE.

I KEEP THINKING ABOUT THE UN'S MAGIC RESETTLEMENT LIST. YOU CAN'T APPLY TO GET ON THE LIST—THEY JUST DECIDE. STILL, SOME PEOPLE START TO CAMP OUT BY THE UN OFFICES, BEGGING WORKERS TO HEAR THEIR CASE. SOME PEOPLE TRY TO PAY BRIBES, LIKE JERI'S DAD. EVEN AFTER THEY'RE DENIED, SOME PEOPLE KEEP TRYING.

I HEARD ABOUT ONE GUY...HIS CASE WAS REJECTED BY THE UN AND HE COULDN'T HANDLE IT. HE...HE KILLED HIMSELF.

ALL OF A SUDDEN, I AM SO JEALOUS AND I WANT TO LEAVE THIS PLACE SO BADLY, I FEEL LIKE I AM GOING TO EXPLODE.

IT'S FUNNY HOW WITHOUT SAYING A WORD, HASSAN IS THE ONE PERSON IN THE WORLD WHO CAN MAKE ME FEEL A LITTLE BETTER.

THANKS.

CHAPTER 9

I **TRY** TO FORGET ABOUT AMERICA.

I TRY TO REMEMBER WHAT FATUMA TOLD ME. THAT GOD HAS A PLAN FOR ME, AND I JUST NEED TO BE PATIENT.

WHEN I HAVE A HARD TIME REMEMBERING...

...FATUMA **MAKES** ME REMEMBER.

I STOP TO GET SOME SAP FROM A TREE. WHEN YOU MIX IT WITH CHARCOAL FROM THE FIRE AND SOME WATER, IT MAKES KIND OF AN INK.

I DON'T GO TO DUGSI VERY OFTEN. BETWEEN ALL MY CHORES AND SCHOOL AND WATCHING HASSAN, IT'S HARD TO FIND THE TIME. BUT IT MAKES FATUMA HAPPY WHEN I GO. BESIDES, IT'S ALMOST RAMADAN.

DUGSI IS WHERE WE GO TO LEARN THE QURAN. WE HAVE THESE LONG BOARDS THAT WE WRITE ON. EVERYONE MAKES THEIR OWN PENS OUT OF BRANCHES, AND YOU WRITE OUT PAGES OF THE QURAN ON THEM—AND THEN WIPE THEM OFF WHEN THEY'RE FULL.

PSSST! WHAT ARE YOU DOING HERE? SIT NEXT TO ME!

OUR IMAM LEADS US IN RECITING A VERSE FROM THE QURAN.

FOR INDEED, WITH HARDSHIP WILL BE EASE.
INDEED, WITH HARDSHIP WILL BE EASE.

I TRY TO HOLD ON TO THIS FEELING OF PEACE WHEN OUR LESSONS ARE OVER.

HEY, ARE YOU GOING TO FAST DURING RAMADAN?

I THINK SO. YOU?

YEAH.

RAMADAN IS OUR HOLY MONTH. FROM SUNRISE TO SUNSET, ALL MUSLIMS ARE SUPPOSED TO REFRAIN FROM EATING AND DRINKING, ALL MONTH. ACTUALLY, IF YOU'RE OLD OR SICK OR TRAVELLING, YOU'RE TECHNICALLY EXEMPT...BUT MOST PEOPLE IN THE CAMPS FAST ANYWAY, EVEN IF THEY'RE SICK OR HUNGRY. A LOT OF KIDS MY AGE DO IT TOO. JUST BECAUSE WE'RE POOR AND HUNGRY DOESN'T MEAN WE CAN'T OBSERVE THE HOLY MONTH.

HEY, BY THE WAY, I'VE GOT AN IDEA FOR HOW WE CAN EARN A LITTLE MONEY DURING RAMADAN. ARE YOU IN?

EVER SINCE THAT DAY IN THE MARKET WITH HIS DAD, JERI HAS BEEN **OBSESSED** WITH MAKING MONEY. LAST WEEK HE MADE US WALK FAR INTO THE BUSH TO FIND FRUITS THAT WE WERE GOING TO SELL AT THE MARKET. EIGHT HOURS LATER, WE EMERGED FROM THE WILDERNESS COVERED WITH SCRATCHES...AND THEN SOME OLDER KIDS CAME AND STOLE ALL OUR FRUIT ANYWAY.

NEEDLESS TO SAY, I'M NOT EXACTLY THRILLED TO HEAR HE HAS A NEW PLAN, BUT AS HIS BEST FRIEND IT'S MY JOB TO HELP HIM OUT.

SO OF COURSE I SAY:

YEAH, I'M IN.

JERI'S IDEA IS PRETTY SIMPLE, AS IT TURNS OUT. HE EXPLAINED IT TO ME ON THE FIRST DAY OF RAMADAN.

LOOK AT ALL THESE WOMEN IN THE MARKET TODAY. WHAT DO YOU THINK THEY'RE SHOPPING FOR?

UH, FOOD?

IFTAR. PEOPLE WANT TO CELEBRATE WITH AN **IFTAR** AT THE END OF THE DAY.

OH. RIGHT. IFTAR.

BACK IN SOMALIA—BACK WHEN, YOU KNOW, WE **HAD** FOOD—A LONG DAY OF FASTING DURING RAMADAN ENDED IN A BIG FEAST WITH YOUR FRIENDS AND FAMILY. IFTAR CELEBRATES THE BREAKING OF THE FAST AT SUNSET. IN SOMALIA, AN IFTAR MIGHT BE FRUITS OR VEGETABLES OR MEAT. HERE IN DADAAB...

I GIVE YOU...

ORANG DRINK

ORANGE DRINK? WHERE'D YOU GET THAT BIG BUCKET? DID YOU STEAL IT?

OF **COURSE** I DIDN'T **STEAL** IT! IT'S RAMADAN, DUMMY! ALI AT THE SWEET SHOP KIND OF...LENT IT TO ME.

LOOK, THIS WHOLE BUCKET COSTS TEN SHILLINGS. WE HAVE TO PAY HIM BACK TWELVE SHILLINGS.

WHAT?! THAT DOESN'T MAKE ANY SENSE! WHY WOULD WE PAY HIM **MORE** THAN WHAT IT'S WORTH?! BESIDES, I DON'T HAVE TWELVE SHILLINGS, AND NEITHER DO YOU!

RELAX! THIS IS OUR WHOLE BUSINESS PLAN!

MOST OF THESE WOMEN DON'T HAVE TEN SHILLINGS EITHER, SO THEY CAN'T BUY A BUCKET OF ORANGE DRINK. BUT THEY COULD SPEND A **FEW** CENTS ON A **FEW** SCOOPS OF MIX— ENOUGH TO MAKE A SPECIAL TREAT FOR THEIR FAMILIES TO CELEBRATE IFTAR...

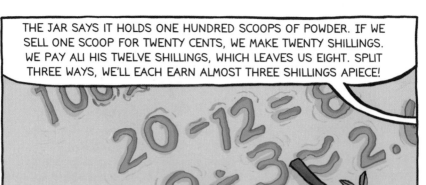

THE JAR SAYS IT HOLDS ONE HUNDRED SCOOPS OF POWDER. IF WE SELL ONE SCOOP FOR TWENTY CENTS, WE MAKE TWENTY SHILLINGS. WE PAY ALI HIS TWELVE SHILLINGS, WHICH LEAVES US EIGHT. SPLIT THREE WAYS, WE'LL EACH EARN ALMOST THREE SHILLINGS APIECE!

AND HERE I THOUGHT **MARYAM** WAS THE MATHEMATICAL GENIUS.

HEY, THAT'S PRETTY GOOD!

THANK YOU. NOW LET'S GET TO WORK!

WHAT A NICE YOUNG MAN!

IT PROBABLY HELPED THAT RAMADAN IS TRADITIONALLY A TIME TO GIVE TO THE POOR AND NEEDY. I THINK A LOT OF THE MUMS BOUGHT DRINK MIX BECAUSE THEY FELT SORRY FOR US. HASSAN WAS ESPECIALLY GOOD AT CHARMING THE WOMEN. BUT WHATEVER THE REASON...

LOOK, FATUMA! NEARLY SIX SHILLINGS! AND THERE WILL BE MORE WHERE THAT CAME FROM TOMORROW!

MY GOODNESS! I CAN BUY SOME TEA AND SUGAR WITH THIS! WE'LL HAVE A REAL IFTAR TOMORROW!

I MISSED SOME SCHOOL DURING RAMADAN...BUT THAT'S JUST PART OF LIFE IN A REFUGEE CAMP. SCHOOL IS IMPORTANT...BUT SO IS SUPPORTING MY FAMILY. I STILL MADE IT TO SCHOOL MOST AFTERNOONS.

BESIDES, WITH THE EXTRA SHILLINGS I WAS EARNING, HASSAN AND I WOULD BE READY TO CELEBRATE WHEN IT WAS TIME FOR...

EID AL-FITR! IT'S ALMOST HERE! I CAN'T WAIT!

THE HOLY MONTH OF RAMADAN ENDS WITH A BIG HOLIDAY— EID AL-FITR. IT'S A DAY OF PRAYER, GIVING TO THE POOR, RELIGIOUS SERMONS, AND...

CANDY!!!

WHEN YOU WAKE UP ON THE FIRST DAY OF EID, YOU START WITH PRAYER.

THEN YOU WASH YOURSELF, BRUSH YOUR TEETH, AND PUT ON NEW CLOTHES IF YOU HAVE THEM. SOME FAMILIES WILL BUY CLOTHES SIX MONTHS IN ADVANCE, AND WON'T WEAR THEM UNTIL EID!

WE DON'T HAVE NEW CLOTHES, BUT I MAKE SURE HASSAN AND I HAVE CLEAN CLOTHES TO WEAR.

JERI DOESN'T HAVE NEW CLOTHES EITHER. NOW THAT I THINK ABOUT IT, HIS SHIRT AND TROUSERS HAVE BIG HOLES IN THEM—I GUESS HE'S HAD THEM FOR A LONG TIME. TODAY THEY ARE CLEAN, THOUGH.

NEXT COMES THE BIG EID PRAYER. USUALLY THAT HAPPENS ON THE FOOTBALL PITCH. IT LOOKS LIKE THERE ARE THOUSANDS OF PEOPLE OUT HERE TODAY, EVEN THOUGH IT'S **HOT**.
I PRAY FOR MY DAD AND MY MUM. I WISH THEY WERE HERE TODAY TO CELEBRATE WITH US.
I PRAY FOR ME AND HASSAN, THAT WE'LL FIND A WAY OUT OF THIS REFUGEE CAMP— THAT SOMEDAY WE'LL FIND A HOME.

AFTER THE PRAYERS ARE OVER—IT'S A HOLIDAY! EID IS REALLY A HOLIDAY FOR KIDS—AND THERE ARE SO MANY KIDS IN THE CAMP. IF YOU ASK A GROWN-UP FOR CANDY OR MONEY...

EID MUBARAK!

...IF THEY HAVE IT, THEY CAN'T SAY NO. IT'S THE **BEST**.

JERI, HASSAN, AND I STUFF OURSELVES SILLY WITH CANDY AND SWEETS ALL DAY LONG. WE SHARE OUR WEALTH WITH THE OTHER KIDS WE SEE. IT FEELS NICE TO BE ABLE TO GIVE SOMETHING TO SOMEONE ELSE FOR A CHANGE.

EID MUBARAK, NIMO!

EID MUBARAK, MARYAM!

EID MUBARAK!

IT'S NICE TO SEE MARYAM WITH HER BROTHERS AND SISTER AGAIN. SHE SEEMS REALLY HAPPY WHEN SHE'S AROUND THEM.

HEY, DO YOU WANT SOME BUBBLE GUM? LET'S HAVE A BUBBLE-BLOWING CONTEST.

I'M IN!

YOU KNOW I COME IN FIRST IN EVERYTHING, RIGHT?

I KNOW MARYAM IS MARRIED NOW...BUT IT'S NICE TO JUST BE KIDS AGAIN FOR A DAY.

THE LAST AND BEST PART OF THE DAY IS THE FEAST. BACK IN SOMALIA, THERE WOULD BE A BIG BANQUET ON EID—FAMILIES WOULD COOK ELABORATE MEALS AND SHARE WITH THEIR NEIGHBOURS. WE STILL DON'T HAVE MUCH FOOD IN THE CAMPS...BUT WHATEVER FOOD PEOPLE DO HAVE, THEY SHARE IT. MEAT, VEGETABLES, FRUITS...NO ONE IS TURNED AWAY FROM THE MEAL.

FOR THE FIRST TIME IN MANY, MANY MONTHS, HASSAN AND I EAT AND EAT UNTIL WE CAN'T FINISH ANOTHER BITE.

MOST PEOPLE IN DADAAB ARE POOR AND STARVING...BUT FOR ONE DAY AT LEAST, NO ONE GOES HUNGRY.

CHAPTER 10

WHEN THE EXCITEMENT OF EID IS OVER, THE BOREDOM OF EVERYDAY LIFE COMES FLOODING BACK. NEEDLESS TO SAY, DISTRACTIONS OF ANY SORT ARE WELCOME IN A REFUGEE CAMP.

C'MON, HASSAN!

TV CREW! AT THE MARKETPLACE! LET'S GO!

HERE'S ONE VERY STRANGE THING ABOUT LIVING IN A REFUGEE CAMP...

SOMETIMES WHITE PEOPLE COME AROUND WITH CAMERAS TO DO REPORTING ON WHAT IT'S LIKE TO LIVE HERE. I GUESS THEY SHOW THESE STORIES ON TV BACK IN ENGLAND OR AUSTRALIA OR AMERICA OR WHEREVER THE REPORTER IS FROM.

WHENEVER WE HEARD THERE WAS A REPORTER IN TOWN, WE'D RUN TO GO WATCH. WHY? WELL, IT WAS SOMETHING TO DO, FOR ONE THING.

FOR ANOTHER THING, SOMETIMES THE REPORTERS OR THE CAMERA PEOPLE WOULD GIVE US CANDY. SCORE!

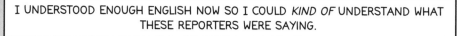

I UNDERSTOOD ENOUGH ENGLISH NOW SO I COULD *KIND OF* UNDERSTAND WHAT THESE REPORTERS WERE SAYING.

<I AM HERE IN DADAAB, A REFUGEE CAMP IN THE MIDDLE OF KENYA, IN AFRICA. DADAAB OPENED IN 1992 AS A TEMPORARY REFUGE FOR SOMALIS FLEEING THE CIVIL WAR IN THEIR COUNTRY. HOWEVER, TEN YEARS LATER, DADAAB SEEMS FAR FROM TEMPORARY, AS THE UNREST IN SOMALIA SHOWS NO SIGN OF SLOWING.>

THE REPORTER WOULD GO ON AND ON, AND TALK ABOUT THE LACK OF WATER, THE LACK OF FOOD, THE POOR HOUSING, AND SO ON.

THEN THE CAMERA CREWS WOULD PACK UP THEIR STUFF...

<SORRY KIDS, WE'RE ALL OUT OF CANDY.>

...AND GET BACK IN THEIR FANCY CARS AND DRIVE OFF IN A CLOUD OF DUST.

I WONDERED IF ANYONE EVER WATCHED THESE SHOWS BACK IN ENGLAND OR AUSTRALIA OR AMERICA. AND IF PEOPLE **DID** WATCH THEM...

WHY WASN'T ANYONE HELPING US?

SOMETIMES REPORTERS OR THE UNITED NATIONS EVEN CAME TO OUR SCHOOL TO CHECK UP ON HOW THINGS WERE RUNNING. YOU COULD ALWAYS TELL WHEN THE UN WAS COMING, BECAUSE THE TEACHERS BROUGHT IN EXTRA CHAIRS AND DESKS TO MAKE IT LOOK LIKE EVERYONE HAD SOMEPLACE TO SIT. THIS GOT ALL THE KIDS TALKING.

GAAL CADAAN!*

THEN THE TEACHERS CONFIRMED IT.

SLAP

GULP

<TOMORROW, I WANT YOUR CLOTHES TO BE SPOTLESS. IF I SEE SO MUCH AS A SPECK OF DIRT ON YOUR TROUSERS, YOU WILL GET IT. **UNDERSTAND?**>

THE NEXT DAY, WE RECITED OUR LESSONS VERRRRRRY CAREFULLY. NO ONE DARED TO MISBEHAVE DURING CLASS— EVEN THOUGH IT WOULD HAVE BEEN REALLY FUNNY TO SEE OUR TEACHERS' FACES IF WE DID.

(*ROUGHLY TRANSLATES TO: "WHITE PEOPLE COMING!")

ON THIS PARTICULAR VISIT, A WHITE LADY GOT UP TO TALK TO US DURING ENGLISH CLASS.

<HELLO, PUPILS. MY NAME IS SUSANA MARTINEZ, AND I AM A SOCIAL WORKER WITH THE UNITED NATIONS. I CAME ALL THE WAY FROM SPAIN TO WORK WITH KIDS HERE IN DADAAB.>

<YOU ARE ALL STRONG, RESILIENT CHILDREN, AND I SEE SO MUCH POTENTIAL IN THIS ROOM. I HOPE YOU'LL KEEP UP WITH YOUR STUDIES. IF YOU HAVE ANY PROBLEMS—AT HOME, OR AT SCHOOL—YOU CAN ALWAYS TALK TO A UN OFFICER. WE ARE HERE TO HELP.>

SOUNDS LIKE SHE TOOK A PAGE FROM MICHAEL'S MOTIVATION 101 SPEECH.

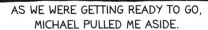
AS WE WERE GETTING READY TO GO, MICHAEL PULLED ME ASIDE.

OMAR, STAY AFTER CLASS FOR A SECOND, WOULD YOU?

SHRUG

<MS. MARTINEZ, THIS IS OMAR, THE STUDENT I WAS TELLING YOU ABOUT.>

<YES, OMAR! IT'S A PLEASURE TO MEET YOU. MICHAEL HAS TOLD ME ABOUT YOUR FAMILY SITUATION. HE SAYS YOU'RE A HARD WORKER, AND THAT YOU'D LIKE TO BE A SOCIAL WORKER WITH THE UNITED NATIONS WHEN YOU GROW UP. IS THAT RIGHT?>

<YES MA'AM.>

MY DREAM SEEMED KIND OF SILLY NOW. HERE WAS AN **ACTUAL** SOCIAL WORKER WITH THE UN...BUT SHE HAD CLEAN CLOTHES AND NICE SHOES. I FELT EXTRA SHABBY NEXT TO HER.

<IT'S HARD ENOUGH KEEPING UP WITH YOUR STUDIES AS A REFUGEE. I IMAGINE IT MUST BE EVEN HARDER FOR YOU, WITHOUT PARENTS AND WITH A YOUNGER BROTHER TO SUPPORT.>

‹IF YOU EVER NEED ANYTHING AT ALL, I AM HERE TO HELP. I WANT TO BE A FRIEND TO YOU IF YOU NEED IT.›

‹YES, MA'AM. THANK YOU, MA'AM.›

‹MICHAEL IS GOING TO KEEP ME UPDATED ON YOUR WORK AT SCHOOL. AND WHO KNOWS—MAYBE WE WILL BE CO-WORKERS SOMEDAY!›

WHAT WAS **THAT** ABOUT?

OH, YOU KNOW. ANOTHER MOTIVATION 101 TALK.

SHE SEEMED NICE, AND LIKE SHE REALLY MEANT WHAT SHE SAID...

BUT I ALSO KNEW THE UN WORKERS LIVED IN A BIG COMPOUND, WITH BIG WALLS TO PROTECT THEM, AND ELECTRICITY AND RUNNING WATER. I KNEW THEY DROVE AROUND THE CAMPS IN BIG FANCY CARS. WHAT DID SHE **REALLY** KNOW ABOUT BEING A REFUGEE?

SCHOOL WENT ON. I JOINED THE DEBATE TEAM. THAT WAS FUN, BECAUSE WE GOT TO DEBATE AGAINST OTHER MIDDLE SCHOOLS IN DADAAB, IN THE OTHER CAMPS. MOSTLY WE DEBATED THINGS LIKE, "THE HUMAN RIGHTS OF THE REFUGEE" AND "WHY EDUCATION IS IMPORTANT FOR BOYS AND GIRLS."...REALLY, IT WAS JUST A WAY TO PRACTISE OUR ENGLISH.

LIFE TAKES ON A ROUTINE, AND DAY AFTER DAY, EVERYTHING STAYED THE SAME. GO TO SCHOOL. CARE FOR HASSAN. DO MY CHORES.

WEEKS AND MONTHS PASSED.

NORMAL. BORING.

WAITING. WAITING.

I'VE LEARNED THAT THE BIGGEST SURPRISES IN LIFE CAN COME WHEN YOU LEAST EXPECT THEM. WHICH IS WHY I WAS COMPLETELY UNPREPARED FOR WHAT WOULD HAPPEN NEXT.

CHAPTER 11

THE DAY STARTED JUST LIKE ANY OTHER.

GRUMBLE GRUMBLE GRUMBLE

ACTUALLY, I REMEMBER WAKING UP **GRUMPIER** THAN MOST DAYS. SLEEPING IN THE DIRT WILL MAKE YOU GRUMPY SOMETIMES.

SOMEONE WOKE UP ON THE WRONG SIDE OF THE BED TODAY!

I DON'T **HAVE** A BED! THAT'S PART OF THE PROBLEM!

JERI AND NIMO COULD TELL I DIDN'T WANT TO BE BOTHERED AND DIDN'T TRY TO TALK TO ME. THEY WERE GOOD LIKE THAT.

ALL DAY AT SCHOOL, IT SEEMED LIKE ANYTHING THAT COULD GO WRONG, DID.

<SURPRISE TEST!>

<SIT UP STRAIGHT!>

√4571
50=

<WE'RE ALL WAITING, YOUNG MAN.>

AND THEN, IN THE MIDDLE OF PRE-ALGEBRA, MY LIFE CHANGED.

OMAR! I NEED TO SPEAK WITH OMAR!

EXCUSE ME, WHAT DO YOU THINK YOU ARE DOING? INTERRUPTING MY CLASS...

IS IT HASSAN? WHAT HAPPENED?

NO...IT'S...NIMO TOO. YOU BOTH HAVE TO COME! YOUR NAMES ARE ON THE LIST. YOU HAVE AN INTERVIEW WITH THE UN FOR RESETTLEMENT!

I NEVER UNDERSTOOD THE PHRASE "TIME STOOD STILL" UNTIL THIS VERY MOMENT. AND NOT JUST TIME— SOUND, MOVEMENT, MY OWN BODY... EVERYTHING JUST STOPPED WORKING.

THEN THROUGH THE SILENCE, I HEARD THE MUFFLED SOUND OF NIMO'S VOICE.

WHAT DO YOU MEAN, **BOTH** OF US?

BOTH! THE UN POSTED A NEW LIST TODAY, AND BOTH OF YOUR NAMES ARE ON THE LIST! TALL SALAN TOLD ME TO COME GET YOU RIGHT AWAY!

OMAR? DID YOU HEAR ME? YOU NEED TO COME WITH ME, RIGHT NOW!

WELL, GO ON. CAN'T KEEP THE UN WAITING. GET OUT OF HERE AND QUIT DISRUPTING MY CLASS!

MY TEACHER WAS A REFUGEE TOO. I WONDERED...WAS HE...JEALOUS?

I GATHERED UP MY THINGS, FEELING NUMB. I FELT EVERY PAIR OF EYES IN THE ROOM ON ME...

...BUT I FELT ONE PAIR OF EYES IN PARTICULAR.

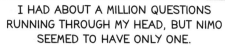
I HAD ABOUT A MILLION QUESTIONS RUNNING THROUGH MY HEAD, BUT NIMO SEEMED TO HAVE ONLY ONE.

WHO ELSE WAS ON THE LIST? ANYONE ELSE FROM OUR BLOCK?

NO ONE ELSE, AS FAR AS I KNOW.

DID THAT UN LADY FROM SPAIN DO THIS?...NO, SHE DIDN'T TALK TO NIMO THAT DAY. AND THAT WAS ONLY A FEW WEEKS AGO. SO WHY **ME**?

THIS ISN'T A **JOKE**, RIGHT? IF THIS IS A JOKE...

IT'S NOT A JOKE! COME ON! EVERYONE'S WAITING FOR YOU AT TALL SALAN'S TENT.

THERE WERE A LOT OF PEOPLE GATHERED AT SALAN'S TENT. HASSAN AND FATUMA WERE THERE TOO.

IS IT TRUE? ARE WE GOING TO AMERICA?

YOU HAVE AN **INTERVIEW**. JUST LIKE ABDIKARIM'S FAMILY, REMEMBER? IT'S JUST A FIRST STEP, NOT A GUARANTEE. AND REMEMBER, LIFE IN AMERICA—OR ENGLAND, OR SWEDEN, OR AUSTRALIA— WON'T BE EASY FOR A REFUGEE...

BUT FATUMA'S DOUBTS WERE DROWNED OUT BY THE CROWD AROUND US.

REMEMBER US WHEN YOU'RE RICH!

YOU'RE GOING TO AMERICA!

YOU'RE GOING TO AMERICA!

THROUGH MY FOGGY HEAD, A LITTLE LIGHT CREEPED IN.

...WE'RE GOING...TO AMERICA?

THEN A MAN GOT UP AND STOOD BY NIMO'S BROTHER. THE CROWD GOT QUIET.

LET ME GIVE YOU SOME ADVICE. I'LL TELL YOU WHAT HAPPENS AT THESE UN INTERVIEWS, SO YOU'RE PREPARED.

THIS WAS ABDIKARIM'S DAD. HIS FAMILY HAD THEIR INTERVIEW TWO MONTHS AGO. THEY WERE WAITING TO HEAR BACK.

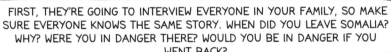

FIRST, THEY'RE GOING TO INTERVIEW EVERYONE IN YOUR FAMILY, SO MAKE SURE EVERYONE KNOWS THE SAME STORY. WHEN DID YOU LEAVE SOMALIA? WHY? WERE YOU IN DANGER THERE? WOULD YOU BE IN DANGER IF YOU WENT BACK?

WE'D ALL BE IN DANGER IF WE WENT BACK!

YOU GOT THAT RIGHT!

MAKE SURE EVERYONE HAS THE SAME ANSWER. THEY'RE LOOKING FOR YOU TO TRIP UP, SO THEY CAN SAY YOUR STORY IS FALSE AND YOU'RE NOT A TRUE REFUGEE.

I LOOKED FOR NIMO, EXPECTING HER TO BE HAPPY ABOUT THAT. IF THERE'S ONE THING THAT MADE NIMO HAPPY, IT WAS MEMORISING FACTS.

BUT SHE DID NOT LOOK HAPPY. SHE LOOKED THE EXACT OPPOSITE OF HAPPY.

HOOYO! HOOYO!

NO, HASSAN. I THINK NIMO AND MARYAM WANT TO BE ALONE RIGHT NOW.

ALL OF A SUDDEN, **I** WANTED TO BE ALONE TOO. BUT PEOPLE KEPT COMING, AND COMING, AND COMING.

WHAT ARE YOU GOING TO SAY? WHEN IS YOUR INTERVIEW? YOU CAN GO TO UNIVERSITY IN AMERICA!

IN THIS WHOLE SEA OF PEOPLE, THERE WAS ONLY ONE PERSON I WANTED TO TALK TO.

BUT I DIDN'T SEE HIM.

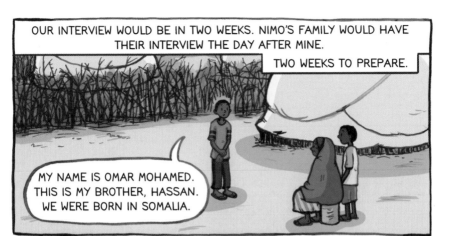

OUR INTERVIEW WOULD BE IN TWO WEEKS. NIMO'S FAMILY WOULD HAVE THEIR INTERVIEW THE DAY AFTER MINE.

TWO WEEKS TO PREPARE.

MY NAME IS OMAR MOHAMED. THIS IS MY BROTHER, HASSAN. WE WERE BORN IN SOMALIA.

THE TOWN YOU ARE FROM...

OH YEAH. WE ARE FROM A SMALL TOWN CALLED MAREEREY.

JERI HASN'T SAID A WORD TO ME SINCE I GOT THE NEWS. I KNOW HE'S FEELING SAD...AND JEALOUS...

...BUT I THOUGHT HE'D BE HAPPY FOR ME TOO.

EVERYONE SAID THAT YOU NEED TO TELL YOUR LIFE STORY AT THIS INTERVIEW. WHAT HAPPENED TO MAKE YOU LEAVE SOMALIA. I HAD BEEN TRYING TO **FORGET** THE PAST, AND TO THINK ABOUT THE FUTURE INSTEAD.

NOW I HAD TO REMEMBER ALL THE TERRIBLE THINGS THAT HAD HAPPENED.

MY NIGHTMARES CAME BACK.

MAMA!

I STILL WENT TO SCHOOL DURING THOSE TWO WEEKS WHILE WE WERE WAITING...BUT IT WAS HARD TO CONCENTRATE ON MY LESSONS.

MY NAME IS OMAR MOHAMED. I WAS BORN IN SOMALIA.

JERI SWITCHED DESKS SO HE WOULDN'T HAVE TO SIT NEXT TO ME. HE WOULDN'T EVEN **LOOK** AT ME. I GUESS I UNDERSTOOD.

BUT I MISSED MY FRIEND. I WISH I COULD TALK TO HIM ABOUT HOW SCARED I WAS.

THE DAY BEFORE OUR INTERVIEW, THERE WAS A LOT TO GET READY.

I WASHED HASSAN'S AND MY BEST OUTFITS. WHEN THEY WERE DRY, I PACKED THEM IN A PLASTIC BAG TO CARRY SO THEY WOULDN'T GET DUSTY ON OUR WALK.

WE TOOK SHOWERS.

WE BRUSHED OUR TEETH, LIKE ALWAYS.

WE'RE GOING ON A LONG WALK TOMORROW. WE'RE GOING TO TALK TO SOME PEOPLE... ABOUT MAYBE GOING TO A NEW HOME.

A **DIFFERENT** HOME. AMERICA.

JUST SAYING THE WORD— **AMERICA**— MADE ME WEAK. I WAS SO NERVOUS.

OUR INTERVIEW WAS FIRST THING TOMORROW MORNING, AND THE UN OFFICES WERE ABOUT AN HOUR'S WALK AWAY. FATUMA THOUGHT WE SHOULD WALK THERE TONIGHT AND SLEEP OUTSIDE THE OFFICE SO THERE'D BE NO CHANCE OF MISSING IT.

OMAR, GO ROLL UP YOUR SLEEPING MAT, WOULD YOU?

OK.

HI.

I HEARD YOU WERE LEAVING TONIGHT.

I THOUGHT YOU'D MAYBE WANT TO BORROW MY LANTERN. IN CASE...I DON'T KNOW, YOU NEED TO FIND A STRANGE BUSH TO PEE IN IN THE MIDDLE OF THE NIGHT.

GOOD LUCK TOMORROW, MY BROTHER.

HE KIND OF RAN OUT OF THERE FAST AFTER THAT, AND I WAS GLAD.
I DIDN'T WANT HIM TO SEE ME CRY.

BUT NOW, AT LEAST, I FELT READY TO GO.

A BUNCH OF OUR NEIGHBOURS WALKED WITH US FOR A WHILE.

I'LL CATCH UP TO YOU, FATUMA.

NIMO'S FAMILY WAS GETTING READY TO LEAVE TOO.

HEY.

HEY.

ARE YOU NERVOUS FOR YOUR INTERVIEW?

OF COURSE I'M NERVOUS. **YOU** KNOW THAT.

OF COURSE I KNEW THAT. OUT OF EVERYONE IN THIS CAMP, NIMO KNEW JUST HOW I WAS FEELING RIGHT NOW.

I FELT LIKE MY WHOLE LIFE DEPENDED ON THIS INTERVIEW.

OMAR...WHY US? OUT OF EVERYONE IN THIS CAMP, WHY **US**? THERE ARE SO MANY PEOPLE WHO DESERVE THIS CHANCE MORE THAN I DO.

SHE DIDN'T SAY IT...BUT I KNEW WHO SHE WAS TALKING ABOUT.

I DON'T KNOW, NIMO.

BUT WHEN GOD GIVES YOU A GIFT, YOU HAVE TO USE IT, RIGHT?

I HAVE TO GO. GOOD LUCK AT YOUR INTERVIEW.

YEAH. YOU TOO.

IT WAS A LONG WALK TO THE UN OFFICE. FATUMA CAN'T WALK TOO QUICKLY, SO IT WOULD TAKE US AN EXTRA LONG TIME.

IT WAS DUSK BY THE TIME WE ARRIVED. I WAS SURPRISED TO SEE LOTS OF PEOPLE CAMPING OUTSIDE THE UN OFFICE.

MOST OF OUR NEIGHBOURS DROPPED OFF AFTER A MILE OR SO. THEN WE WERE ON OUR OWN.

DOES **EVERYONE** HAVE AN INTERVIEW TOMORROW?

I WENT TO FETCH SOME WATER. WE ATE THE ANJEERA FATUMA HAD MADE FOR OUR TRIP.

WE UNROLLED OUR SLEEPING MATS.

HOOYO!

HASSAN WAS EXCITED BY THE WALK AND THE NEW LOCATION AND ALL THE NEW PEOPLE. IT WAS HARD TO CALM HIM DOWN FOR SLEEP. MY STORIES DIDN'T HELP THIS TIME.

LIE DOWN, HASSAN, AND I'LL TELL YOU A STORY ABOUT WHEN I WAS A LITTLE GIRL IN SOMALIA.

WHEN I WAS A LITTLE GIRL, WE LIVED IN A REMOTE VILLAGE. BUT ONE DAY, MY FATHER TOOK OUR FAMILY ON A TRIP TO MOGADISHU.
BACK THEN, MOGADISHU WAS A BUSTLING CITY. A PEACEFUL CITY, WITH FOOD TO BUY ON EVERY CORNER.
YOU COULD STILL SEE ALL THE PALACES, MOSQUES, AND MINARETS FROM ANCIENT TIMES.
IT WAS THE FIRST TIME I'D EVER SEEN THE OCEAN. IT WAS SO BLUE. A DIFFERENT BLUE FROM THE SKY. AND THE AIR SMELLED LIKE SALT.
THE OCEAN SEEMED TO GO ON FOREVER.

I TRIED TO IMAGINE WAVES OF WATER INSTEAD OF THE WAVES OF SAND SURROUNDING US.
I TRIED TO SMELL SALT IN THE DUSTY WIND THAT BLEW OVER US.
I THINK FATUMA HELPED A LOT OF PEOPLE FALL ASLEEP THAT NIGHT.

CHAPTER 12

I GOT UP EARLY THE NEXT MORNING—THE SOUND OF PEOPLE GETTING READY ALL AROUND ME WOKE ME UP.

I GOT US WATER.
WE BRUSHED OUR TEETH.
WE PUT ON OUR CLEAN CLOTHES.

VERY HANDSOME!

WE WAITED.

AS THE SUN GOT HIGHER, PEOPLE GOT MORE AND MORE ANXIOUS. THEY STARTED CROWDING THE DOOR, AFRAID THEY'D BE OVERLOOKED.

FINALLY, THE DOOR OPENED. PEOPLE STARTED PUSHING AND SCRAMBLING TO GET TO THE FRONT OF THE LINE. .

JUST STAY WITH ME, BOYS. DON'T WORRY. WE HAVE AN APPOINTMENT. WE WILL BE SEEN. EVERYTHING WILL BE OK.

WE STEPPED INTO A BIG WAITING AREA. I DON'T KNOW HOW SO MANY PEOPLE WERE ALREADY THERE.

EVERYONE LOOKED NERVOUS.

EVERY SO OFTEN, A UN WORKER WOULD OPEN A DOOR AND SAY...

SAYYID FARAH.

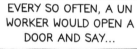

ABDULLAHI MIRE.

OMAR MOHAMED AND HASSAN MOHAMED.

SUDDENLY I FELT LIKE MY LEGS WOULD FOLD UP UNDER ME. I FORCED MYSELF TO STAND UP. IT HELPED TO HOLD ON TO HASSAN AND FATUMA.

UNH
The UN R

WE WALKED INTO THE OFFICE.

<HAVE A SEAT. MY NAME IS DAVID. I WORK FOR THE UNITED NATIONS. I'LL BE CONDUCTING YOUR INITIAL INTERVIEW.>

ENGLISH! I DIDN'T KNOW THE INTERVIEW WOULD BE IN **ENGLISH!** HOW WAS I SUPPOSED TO...

<THIS IS SALAT. HE'LL BE YOUR INTERPRETER.>

HE SAID, HIS NAME IS DAVID. HE WORKS FOR THE UNITED NATIONS AND HE'LL CONDUCT YOUR INITIAL INTERVIEW. MY NAME IS SALAT AND I'LL BE YOUR INTERPRETER.

WHEW!

IT TOOK A WHILE TO TALK. FIRST THE UN GUY ASKED A QUESTION. THEN THE INTERPRETER REPEATED IT IN SOMALI. THEN I ANSWERED IN SOMALI. THEN THE INTERPRETER REPEATED IT IN ENGLISH.

<WHAT IS YOUR NAME?>

MAGACAA?

MAGACEYKU WAA CUMAR MOHAMED.

<MY NAME IS OMAR MOHAMED.>

<REMEMBER, THIS IS NOT A **TRIAL**. THERE ARE NO RIGHT OR WRONG ANSWERS. WE JUST NEED TO GET A FILE STARTED TO SEE IF YOU ARE ELIGIBLE FOR RESETTLEMENT. DO YOU UNDERSTAND?>

I WONDERED IF THE UN WORKER HAD EVER SMILED IN HIS ENTIRE LIFE. I WISH SUSANA MARTINEZ WERE HERE.

Y...YES. I UNDERSTAND.

<JUST ANSWER HONESTLY AND COMPLETELY, AND EVERYTHING WILL BE FINE. LET'S BEGIN.>

<WHERE WERE YOU BORN?>

I WAS BORN IN THE SMALL TOWN OF MAREEREY IN SOMALIA. IT'S A RURAL AREA. OUR FATHER WAS A FARMER.

<WHAT DO YOU REMEMBER OF YOUR HOME?>

I WAS ONLY A LITTLE KID, BUT I REMEMBER...

...GREEN.
I REMEMBER THE COLOUR GREEN.
I REMEMBER MY DAD USED TO TAKE ME OUT TO THE FIELDS WITH HIM WHILE HE WORKED. MY MOTHER WOULD BRING HIM LUNCH, AND WE'D ALL EAT TOGETHER UNDER A TREE.

<WHY DID YOUR FAMILY LEAVE SOMALIA?>

...

<OMAR? WHAT DO YOU REMEMBER HAPPENING ON THE DAY YOU LEFT YOUR HOME?>

I'D PRACTICED THIS STORY MANY TIMES IN MY HEAD. I DIDN'T REALISE HOW HARD IT WOULD BE TO SAY THE WORDS OUT LOUD, TO THIS UNFRIENDLY MAN IN THIS STRANGE ROOM.

<YOUNG MAN...>

I REMEMBER...

MY TOYS. I WAS PLAYING UNDER A TREE WITH MY TOYS. I LOVED THOSE TOYS. MY DAD MADE THEM FOR ME. I USED TO BUILD HOUSES WITH THEM.

<AND THEN...?>

AND THEN...

...THE MEN CAME. I DIDN'T KNOW THEM—I'D NEVER SEEN THEM BEFORE. THEY WALKED OUT INTO THE FIELD AND STARTED TALKING WITH MY FATHER.

THEY STARTED YELLING. AND THEN...

BANG!

BANG!

BANG!

I RAN BACK TOWARD OUR HOUSE. MY MOTHER WAS WALKING TO THE FIELDS, CARRYING LUNCH FOR ME AND MY FATHER. SHE HAD HASSAN WITH HER.

I HAD A HARD TIME TELLING HER WHAT HAPPENED—I WAS SO LITTLE. BUT SHE SEEMED TO UNDERSTAND RIGHT AWAY THAT SOMETHING BAD HAD HAPPENED.

MAMA!

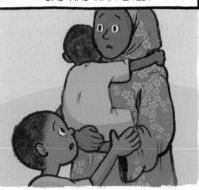

TAKE YOUR BROTHER, OMAR. RUN AS FAST AS YOU CAN BACK TO OUR VILLAGE. GO TO SADIYA'S HOUSE NEXT DOOR. SHE'LL TAKE CARE OF YOU UNTIL I COME BACK.

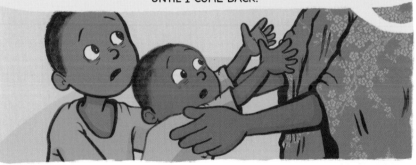

DON'T BE SCARED, MY BRAVE BOY. I NEED YOU TO TAKE CARE OF YOUR BROTHER. I WILL COME BACK TO YOU AS SOON AS I CAN.

EVERYTHING WILL BE OK.

181

OUR HOUSE AND OUR VILLAGE WAS FAR FROM OUR FIELDS. HASSAN COULDN'T WALK VERY FAST AT ALL. WE BARELY MADE IT TO MY NEIGHBOUR'S HOUSE BEFORE...

OMAR! HASSAN! GET INSIDE, QUICKLY! WE'VE HEARD RUMOURS...

THEN I HEARD GUNSHOTS. AND SCREAMING. AND SOON THE WHOLE VILLAGE WAS RUNNING. THERE WERE ANGRY MEN EVERYWHERE.

RUN, OMAR! RUN!

MAMA? WHERE IS MAMA?

MAMA!

RUN!

WE RAN. EVERY DIRECTION WE TURNED, WE FOUND MORE FIGHTING. WE RAN, AND WE RAN, AND WE RAN.

HUSH, OMAR! YOU MUST BE QUIET!

I WANT MAMA!

<WHAT HAPPENED TO YOUR MOTHER?>

I...

<DID SHE FIND YOU?>

RUN!

<DO YOU KNOW WHAT HAPPENED TO HER?>

NO, SIR.

<DO YOU HAVE ANY IDEA ABOUT YOUR MOTHER'S WHEREABOUTS TODAY? IS SHE ALIVE, OR IS SHE...>

MAMA!

I DON'T KNOW, SIR.
I DON'T KNOW.
I DON'T KNOW.
I DON'T KNOW.

PLEASE. THE BOY NEEDS A BREAK.

<ALL RIGHT. WE'LL BE BACK IN FIVE MINUTES.>

WHY DIDN'T SHE FIND US?

I DON'T KNOW.

WHAT HAPPENED TO HER? WHERE **IS** SHE?

I DON'T KNOW. I DON'T KNOW. I DON'T KNOW.

I KNOW...SHE LOVED YOU. A MOTHER ALWAYS DOES.

HOOYO.

AHEM
‹I BROUGHT YOU SOMETHING TO DRINK. SOME JUICE.›

SNIFF

SNIFF MY JUICE FEELS FUNNY. IT'S..

...COLD!

UM... YES.

IT MAY SOUND WEIRD, BUT THAT WAS THE FIRST COLD DRINK I'D EVER HAD IN MY ENTIRE LIFE.

AHEM ‹SHALL WE CONTINUE?›

I THINK HE WAS TRYING TO...SMILE?

YES.

I'M READY.

185

I TOLD THE MAN HOW WE WALKED WITH OUR NEIGHBOURS FOR DAYS... WEEKS. IT'S FUNNY, WE'D NEVER SPENT THAT MUCH TIME WITH OUR NEIGHBOURS BEFORE, BUT NOW...THEY HAD OUR LIVES IN THEIR HANDS.

OUR NEIGHBOUR SADIYA TOOK CARE OF US, EVEN THOUGH SHE WAS VERY OLD. SHE NEVER LEFT US BEHIND.

WE WALKED AND WALKED AND WALKED...BUT THERE WAS NO PLACE TO GO. THERE WAS TOO MUCH FIGHTING. WHAT HAPPENED IN OUR VILLAGE WAS HAPPENING **EVERYWHERE** IN SOMALIA. WE HAD TO FIND SOMEPLACE SAFE.

OUR GROUP COULDN'T TRAVEL VERY FAST— IT WAS MOSTLY OLDER PEOPLE, OR MUMS WITH YOUNG CHILREN. BUT WE WALKED AS FAST AS WE COULD.

AS WE WALKED, WE MET MORE AND MORE PEOPLE WHO WERE RUNNING FROM THEIR HOMES. WE DIDN'T KNOW WHERE WE WERE GOING, BUT WE ALL KEPT WALKING. ONE FOOT IN FRONT OF THE OTHER.

SOMEONE IN THE GROUP HAD HEARD ABOUT A PLACE IN KENYA. A SAFE PLACE FOR SOMALIS TO GO. IT WAS RUN BY THE UNITED NATIONS. SO THE GROWN-UPS DECIDED WE SHOULD LEAVE OUR COUNTRY AND GO THERE.

WE FOLLOWED SIGNS LEFT BY OTHER SOMALIS. A BENT TREE BRANCH MEANT, TURN HERE.

WE HID IN BUSHES WHEN WE HEARD FIGHTING.

SOMETIMES WE COULDN'T HIDE, AND THE BANDITS FOUND US. THEY'D TAKE OUR FOOD, OUR CLOTHES...OUR...EVERYTHING.

I WAS YOUNG, BUT...I KNEW PEOPLE WERE DYING. OUR GROUP GOT SMALLER AND SMALLER.

OUR NEIGHBOUR SADIYA...SHE TOOK CARE OF US FOR AS LONG AS SHE COULD, BUT...SHE DIDN'T MAKE IT.

OTHERS IN OUR GROUP MUST HAVE KEPT CARING FOR ME AND HASSAN, BUT I DON'T REMEMBER MUCH OF THAT.

AS WE WALKED, I GOT WEAKER...

AND WEAKER...

AND WEAKER.

JUST AS I WAS FADING INTO NOTHING, WE MADE IT TO THE CAMP. I DON'T REMEMBER MUCH ABOUT THAT, EITHER.

I KNOW THAT SO MANY SOMALIS WERE FLEEING THE COUNTRY BECAUSE OF THE CIVIL WAR, WE WERE ALL AUTOMATICALLY REGISTERED AS REFUGEES. THERE WERE TOO MANY OF US TO GO ONE BY ONE.

THE UN OFFICIALS SEPARATED HASSAN AND ME FROM OUR GROUP. THEY SAID WE WERE SICK AND WE NEEDED TO STAY IN THE HOSPITAL.

FOR ME, THE FIRST YEARS ARE LOST.

I FELT LIKE I WAS FADING IN AND OUT. LIKE I BARELY EXISTED. MAYBE I WAS A GHOST. HASSAN TOO.

MALNOURISHED.

MALARIA.

SICK.

DEHYDRATED.

WE SPENT A LONG TIME IN THE HOSPITAL.

SLOWLY, WE STARTED TO FADE BACK IN.

THE NURSES HAD TO TEACH ME HOW TO WALK AGAIN. FUNNY, AFTER WE'D WALKED SO FAR, I HAD TO LEARN AGAIN.

WHEN WE WERE BETTER, A UN WORKER BROUGHT US TO OUR NEW HOME.

BOYS, THIS IS FATUMA. SINCE YOU ARRIVED WITHOUT PARENTS, FATUMA WILL CARE FOR YOU. THINK OF HER AS...YOUR FOSTER MUM.

I...I DIDN'T LIKE FATUMA AT FIRST.

...SORRY, FATUMA.

I WANTED MY MUM.

I DIDN'T LIKE THE FOOD WE HAD TO EAT.

FLING

NO!

I WAS USED TO EATING MEAT AND VEGETABLES FROM OUR FARM. NOW THE UN GAVE US FLOUR AND OIL AND NO ONE KNEW HOW TO USE IT. SOME PEOPLE THOUGHT THE FLOUR WAS POWDERED MILK. THEY MIXED IT WITH WATER AND GAVE IT TO THEIR CHILDREN AND...SOME OF THEM DIED.

‹AND WHAT ABOUT HASSAN? WHEN DID YOU LEARN ABOUT HIS DISABILITIES?›

WELL...HASSAN WAS ALWAYS DIFFERENT FROM OTHER KIDS HIS AGE. HE DIDN'T TALK. AND HE HAD REALLY BAD TANTRUMS. HE COULD SCREAM AND KICK FOR HOURS WITHOUT GETTING TIRED.

I WAS THE ONLY ONE WHO COULD CALM HIM DOWN.

SHHH, HASSAN. IT'S OK. I'M RIGHT HERE. I'M NOT LEAVING. I'M RIGHT HERE.

BUT AS HE GOT OLDER, I...I COULDN'T ALWAYS HELP HIM. HE STARTED HAVING SEIZURES. THAT'S WHAT THE DOCTORS CALLED THEM. HE WOULD FALL TO THE GROUND AND HIS BODY WOULD START JERKING AROUND AND I COULDN'T STOP IT.

FATUMA! HELP!

FATUMA TOOK HIM TO THE HOSPITAL, BUT THE DOCTORS DIDN'T KNOW WHAT TO DO.

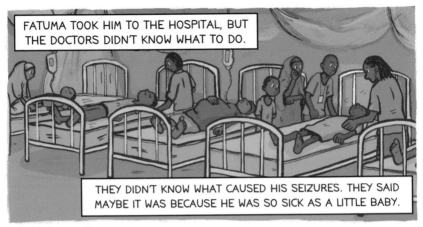

THEY DIDN'T KNOW WHAT CAUSED HIS SEIZURES. THEY SAID MAYBE IT WAS BECAUSE HE WAS SO SICK AS A LITTLE BABY.

THEY DIDN'T HAVE ANY MEDICINE TO GIVE HIM TO MAKE THEM STOP.

THEY SAID THE BEST WE COULD DO WOULD BE TO WATCH HIM CONSTANTLY, AND MAKE SURE HE DIDN'T BITE OFF HIS TONGUE WHILE HE WAS HAVING A SEIZURE.

WORD SPREAD AMONGST OUR NEIGHBOURS, AND SOON EVERYONE WAS STOPPING IN TO GIVE THEIR ADVICE TO FATUMA.

HE'S NOT EVEN YOUR **REAL** SON, FATUMA.

HE'S JUST GOING TO GET MORE AND MORE VIOLENT AS HE GETS OLDER.

TELL THE UN YOU'VE CHANGED YOUR MIND ABOUT BEING A FOSTER MUM.

WHAT YOU NEED TO DO, FATUMA, IS KEEP THE BOY TIED UP. THAT WAY HE WON'T HARM YOU OR OTHERS...

GET OUT! ALL OF YOU! TIE A BOY UP, ARE YOU **CRAZY**?! HE IS LIKE MY OWN SON, AND I WILL TREAT HIM AS SUCH.

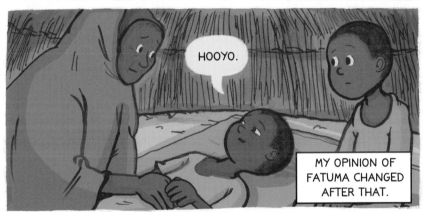

HOOYO.

MY OPINION OF FATUMA CHANGED AFTER THAT.

THE NEXT TIME HASSAN HAD A SEIZURE, FATUMA WAS RIGHT THERE NEXT TO HIM, HOLDING DOWN HIS TONGUE, ROCKING HIM AND SINGING TO HIM.

FATUMA?

...WHY DO YOU WANT TO BE OUR FOSTER MUM? WOULDN'T YOUR LIFE BE EASIER WITHOUT US? WHY ARE YOU BEING SO NICE TO US?

YOU REMIND ME OF MY OWN CHILDREN. I HAD FOUR BOYS OF MY OWN, YOU KNOW.

YOU DO? WHERE ARE THEY NOW?

THEY WERE KILLED IN SOMALIA. BUT THEY WERE GOOD BOYS. SWEET BOYS. JUST LIKE THE TWO OF YOU.

FATUMA STILL TAKES CARE OF US. THE UN NAMED HER OUR LEGAL GUARDIAN.

BY NOW, I HAD BEEN TALKING FOR A LONG, LONG TIME. I WAS EXHAUSTED. BUT THE UN OFFICER STILL ASKED QUESTION AFTER QUESTION AFTER QUESTION. FINALLY...

<VERY WELL. I HAVE EVERYTHING I NEED TO OPEN YOUR FILE. SOMEONE WILL CONTACT YOU IF WE NEED ADDITIONAL INFORMATION. A UN OFFICER WILL REVIEW YOUR CASE WITHIN TWO TO FOUR MONTHS AND DECIDE IF YOU MEET THE REQUIREMENTS FOR RESETTLEMENT. IF YOU DO, YOU WILL BE CALLED BACK FOR A SECOND INTERVIEW WITH THE UNITED NATIONS. GOOD DAY.>

AND JUST LIKE THAT, WE WERE OUTSIDE AGAIN. THE SUN WAS SO BRIGHT AFTER BEING INSIDE ALL DAY...MY KNEES FELT SO WEAK...

SLUMP

ALL AROUND US, OTHER FAMILIES WERE CRYING. SOME JUST LOOKED SHOCKED. I GUESS LIKE ME, THEY HAD JUST RE-LIVED THE WORST DAYS OF THEIR LIVES.

FATUMA, HASSAN, AND I SLEPT UNDER A TREE BY THE UN THAT NIGHT. WE DIDN'T FEEL UP TO MAKING THE TRIP HOME JUST THEN.
UNHCR
WE WOKE UP EARLY THE NEXT MORNING TO START WALKING. AS WE WERE LEAVING...
OMAR! WE JUST GOT HERE! OUR INTERVIEW IS IN A FEW HOURS. HOW DID IT GO?
IT'S...OVER.
I'LL...SEE YOU IN SCHOOL, I GUESS.
YEAH. SEE YOU IN SCHOOL.

CHAPTER 13

OVER THE NEXT FEW WEEKS, NEIGHBOURS AND FRIENDS KEPT STOPPING BY TO ASK HOW THE INTERVIEW WENT.

YOU'RE GOING TO **AMERICA!**

AT SCHOOL, KIDS KEPT BOTHERING ME AND NIMO ABOUT IT.

YOU'RE GOING TO AMERICA!

BRING ME IN YOUR SUITCASE!

HEY, I'M HIS BEST FRIEND. IF ANYONE GETS TO HIDE IN HIS SUITCASE, IT'S ME!

WHAT IF...THEY DON'T PICK ME? I DIDN'T HAVE ANSWERS FOR A LOT OF THE QUESTIONS. I THINK I DID A BAD JOB IN THE INTERVIEW.

YOU'LL GO. YOU KNOW THEY SAY THE PEOPLE WITH THE REALLY BAD STORIES ARE THE ONES WHO GET RESETTLED. YOU'RE AN ORPHAN! YOUR LITTLE BROTHER HAS A DISABILITY! WHO COULD HAVE A WORSE STORY THAN **YOU**?

WAITING WAS HARD...BUT EVERYONE SEEMED SO SURE THAT I WAS ABOUT TO BE SENT OFF TO AMERICA.

I BEGAN TO IMAGINE, JUST A LITTLE, WHAT LIFE IN AMERICA WOULD BE LIKE FOR HASSAN, FATUMA AND ME.

I KEPT GOING TO SCHOOL, OF COURSE—I DIDN'T WANT TO BE **TOO** FAR BEHIND IN MY CLASSES WHEN I STARTED SCHOOL IN AMERICA.

I WONDER WHAT SCHOOL IS LIKE IN AMERICA. I WONDER WHAT KIND OF CLASSES I'LL TAKE.

SO...MAYBE I DIDN'T STUDY **QUITE** AS HARD IN SCHOOL AS I COULD HAVE. BUT WHY SHOULD I WORRY ABOUT SCHOOL WHEN I'D BE IN AMERICA BY THE END OF THE YEAR?

FOR A MONTH AFTER THE INTERVIEW, I DIDN'T WORRY TOO MUCH. AFTER ALL, THE UN WORKER SAID IT WOULD TAKE TWO TO FOUR MONTHS TO HEAR ANYTHING.

BUT AFTER TWO MONTHS OF WAITING...

I STARTED TO GO A LITTLE...CRAZY.

I GOT REALLY JUMPY. AT SCHOOL, EVERY TIME SOMEONE CAME THROUGH THE DOOR, I WAS SURE IT WAS A NEIGHBOUR COMING TO TELL ME MY NAME WAS ON THE LIST FOR A SECOND INTERVIEW.

I STARTED TO FEEL SICK ALL THE TIME.

AND NERVOUS.

JUST WAITING.

AND WAITING.

AND WAITING.

NOTHING.

MAYBE HASSAN COULD FEEL MY ANXIETY...BECAUSE SOON AFTER, HASSAN HAD ANOTHER SEIZURE. IT HAD BEEN **TWO YEARS** SINCE HIS LAST ONE. YET AGAIN, THE DOCTORS WEREN'T SURE WHAT CAUSED IT OR HOW TO HELP HIM. THEY SAID TO WAIT AND SEE.

I'M SORRY, HASSAN. IF ONLY I'D DONE BETTER IN OUR INTERVIEW, WE'D BE GOING TO AMERICA. THE DOCTORS IN AMERICA COULD STOP YOUR SEIZURES, I KNOW IT.

IN A REFUGEE CAMP, IT FELT LIKE ALL YOU EVER DID WAS **WAIT**.

WAIT TO SEE IF YOUR BROTHER GETS WELL AGAIN.

WAIT FOR WATER. WAIT FOR FOOD.

WAIT TO HEAR FROM THE UNITED NATIONS.
WAIT FOR YOUR LIFE TO START.
JERI, ARE YOU READY?
HOW MANY TIMES HAVE I TOLD YOU NOT TO INTERFERE IN MATTERS BETWEEN ME AND YOUR MOTHER? NOW GET OUT OF HERE, LIMPY!
WAIT FOR YOUR LIFE TO GET BETTER.
EVERY SINGLE PERSON IN THIS CAMP WAS WAITING FOR SOMETHING BETTER.
WAITING.
WAITING.
SNIFF
WAITING.
HOW LONG CAN YOU WAIT BEFORE YOU LOSE ALL HOPE?

CHAPTER 14

AS I STARTED EIGHTH GRADE I EVENTUALLY THOUGHT LESS...

AND LESS...

ABOUT AMERICA.

LIKE I SAID, IN A REFUGEE CAMP, LIFE GOES ON. I KEPT MYSELF BUSY. I HAD A NEW CLASS AND NEW TEACHERS TO OCCUPY MY THOUGHTS.

HASSAN HADN'T HAD ANOTHER SEIZURE. HE SEEMED TO BE HAPPY, CARING FOR BROWNIE AND HELPING MARYAM.

BUT WHENEVER I THOUGHT I'D FORGOTTEN ABOUT AMERICA...

SOMETHING WOULD REMIND ME.

OMAR! WAKE UP! I HAVE GOOD NEWS!

ARE WE BEING RESETTLED? WE'RE GOING TO AMERICA?

AMERICA? NO. IT'S BROWNIE. SHE'S **PREGNANT**!

BROWNIE? THE...GOAT?

YES! THAT MEANS WE'LL HAVE THREE OR FOUR GOATS TO MILK SOON, GOD WILLING!

...WHERE ARE YOU GOING?

I'M GOING TO FETCH THE WATER!

I GOT SO ANGRY ALL OF A SUDDEN. ANGRY AT MYSELF FOR GETTING MY HOPES UP. I WAS STILL STUCK HERE, AND I WAS SUPPOSED TO BE HAPPY ABOUT SOME STUPID **GOATS**?

HOOYO!

NO! YOU STAY HERE! YOU'LL JUST SLOW ME DOWN. I'M **TIRED** OF YOU SLOWING ME DOWN!

I TRIED NOT TO SEE THE HURT AND SURPRISED LOOK ON HASSAN'S FACE.

PANT PANT
OMAR!

NIMO?

OMAR! MY FAMILY GOT OUR SECOND INTERVIEW! DID YOU GET YOURS TOO? DO YOU THINK IT'S REALLY HAPPENING—THAT WE'RE GOING TO AMERICA? I NEVER THOUGHT IT WOULD **REALLY** HAPPEN...

HOW DID YOU HEAR ABOUT YOUR INTERVIEW? **WHO TOLD YOU?**
TALL SALAN TOLD MY BROTHER LAST NIGHT...OMAR? WHERE ARE YOU GOING?
SIR! SIR! I HEARD NIMO'S FAMILY WAS ON THE LIST FOR A SECOND INTERVIEW! WAS I...DID WE...
NO, OMAR. I DIDN'T HEAR ANYTHING FROM THE UN OFFICER ABOUT YOUR CASE.
ARE YOU SURE? MAYBE...
THE ONLY NAMES ON THE LIST THIS WEEK WERE NIMO'S FAMILY, AND ABDIKARIM'S.
MY FOOTBALL FRIEND. SO HIS FAMILY HAD A SECOND INTERVIEW TOO.
A NEW LIST COMES OUT EVERY WEEK. AS A COMMUNITY LEADER, I ALWAYS FIND OUT IF SOMEONE HERE IS ON THE LIST. I'LL SEND WORD THE MOMENT I HEAR ANYTHING.

THAT FEVER THAT I THOUGHT HAD GONE AWAY...IT FIRED UP INSIDE ME AND TOOK HOLD OF ME AGAIN, WORSE THAN EVER. GOING TO AMERICA BECAME ALL I COULD THINK ABOUT.

I'M **SURE** WE'LL BE ON THE LIST NEXT WEEK! THEY CAN PROBABLY ONLY DO A CERTAIN NUMBER OF INTERVIEWS PER WEEK. OUR NAMES MUST BE NEXT ON THE LIST!

BUT OUR NAMES WEREN'T ON THE LIST THE NEXT WEEK.

OR THE NEXT.

OR THE NEXT.

I SLID DEEPER AND DEEPER INTO A DARK HOLE. NOT ONLY THAT, BUT I FELT LIKE I HAD A DARKNESS GROWING INSIDE ME TOO. IT MADE ME FEEL ANGRY AND MEAN, AND I TOOK IT OUT ON THE PEOPLE I LOVED MOST.

I COULD BARELY LOOK AT NIMO ANYMORE, LET ALONE TALK TO HER. I PRETENDED I DIDN'T NOTICE THAT SHE WAS QUIETER AND SADDER THAN I'D EVER SEEN HER.

I PRETENDED NOT TO KNOW WHEN HER FAMILY WENT FOR HER SECOND INTERVIEW...OR THEIR THIRD. I PRETENDED NOT TO LISTEN WHEN KIDS AT SCHOOL ASKED HER ABOUT IT.

WHEN DO YOU LEAVE FOR AMERICA?

WE'RE NOT GOING TO AMERICA...WE'RE BEING RESETTLED TO CANADA.

I HAVE TO GO.

WAIT! OMAR!

PLEASE, TALK TO ME! I'M SORRY IT'S ME AND NOT YOU! I'M SORRY IT'S NOT MARYAM! IT'S NOT FAIR. **PLEASE**, OMAR. FORGIVE ME.

I PRETENDED NOT TO SEE SHE WAS TORN UP INSIDE WITH GUILT.

I TURNED MY BACK ON HER.

I PRETENDED NOT TO KNOW THAT I PUT JERI IN A TOUGH SPOT, BETWEEN US.

SHE REALLY DOES FEEL BAD, YOU KNOW. IF YOU JUST TELL HER YOU'RE HAPPY FOR HER, THAT YOU DON'T BLAME HER FOR ANYTHING...

SURE. LIKE THAT WAS EASY FOR **YOU** TO DO WHEN YOU THOUGHT **I** WAS GOING TO AMERICA. NOW THAT I'M STUCK HERE, ALL OF A SUDDEN YOU'RE FULL OF GOOD ADVICE.

MAYBE YOU'RE NOT STUCK HERE. MAYBE YOU'LL STILL GO. THE UN—

SHUT UP! YOU KNOW IT'S NOT TRUE! IT'S BEEN MONTHS NOW. AND WHAT'S MORE...

I FELT THE MEANNESS BILLOW UP INSIDE ME.

WHAT'S MORE, YOU'RE **HAPPY** I'M NOT GOING TO AMERICA! YOU'RE **GLAD** I'M STUCK HERE IN THIS REFUGEE CAMP WITH YOU!

I'M TRYING TO MAKE YOU FEEL **BETTER**! I'M YOUR **FRIEND**! THAT'S MORE THAN I CAN SAY FOR YOU! I HAVEN'T EVEN HAD **ONE** INTERVIEW YET, AND YOU DON'T EVEN **CARE**!

I WAS SPREADING THE DARKNESS AROUND ME, INFECTING EVERYONE IN MY PATH.
AND THE PERSON I CARED ABOUT MOST IN THE WORLD GOT THE WORST OF IT.
HASSAN ALMOST ALWAYS HELPS WITH THE CHORES THESE DAYS. BUT NOW, WHEN I FEEL SO ANGRY...I GET IMPATIENT.
NO, HASSAN. GO BACK HOME. STAY WITH FATUMA.
GO!
LEAVE ME ALONE!
GO!

HASSAN? OMAR? WHAT'S GOING ON HERE? ARE YOU TWO FIGHTING?

IT'S NONE OF YOUR BUSINESS, MARYAM.

IT **IS** MY BUSINESS IF YOU'RE BEING MEAN TO **EVERYONE** IN THIS BLOCK, JUST BECAUSE YOU'RE ANGRY.

YOU DON'T UNDERSTAND! YOU DON'T KNOW WHAT IT'S LIKE TO BE SO CLOSE TO YOUR DREAMS AND THEN... AND THEN...

AND THEN, IT'S AS IF THE DARKNESS IS SWEPT FROM MY EYES, AND FOR THE FIRST TIME IN WEEKS I NOTICE SOMEONE BESIDES MYSELF.

MARYAM. YOUR BELLY. YOU'RE...

THE ANGER AND THE FIGHT SEEMED TO LEAVE ALL THREE OF US AT ONCE.

LIFE ISN'T FAIR.

BUT I KNOW...YOUR DAUGHTER WILL BE LUCKY, BECAUSE SHE'LL HAVE YOU FOR A MUM.

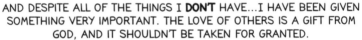

I THOUGHT BACK TO WHAT JERI TOLD ME, YEARS AGO. NONE OF US ASK TO BE BORN **WHERE** WE ARE, OR **HOW** WE ARE. THE CHALLENGE OF LIFE IS TO MAKE THE MOST OUT OF WHAT YOU'VE BEEN GIVEN.

AND DESPITE ALL OF THE THINGS I **DON'T** HAVE...I HAVE BEEN GIVEN SOMETHING VERY IMPORTANT. THE LOVE OF OTHERS IS A GIFT FROM GOD, AND IT SHOULDN'T BE TAKEN FOR GRANTED.

I'M SORRY, HASSAN. I'M SORRY, MARYAM.

C'MON. LET'S GO TALK TO NIMO.

NIMO MET US AT THE SWING, FOR OLD TIMES' SAKE.

SO. YOU'RE REALLY GOING TO CANADA.

YEAH.

I NEVER THOUGHT I'D BE GOING WITHOUT YOU, MARYAM.

LOOK ON THE BRIGHT SIDE— NOW YOU CAN PAINT YOUR BEDROOM GREEN LIKE YOU WANTED.

STOP JOKING! IT ISN'T **FUNNY**! I DON'T CARE ABOUT A STUPID **COLOUR**!

I KNOW, NIMO. I KNOW.

IT'S NOT FAIR. NONE OF THIS IS FAIR.
IT SHOULD BE YOU, MARYAM. OR YOU, OMAR.
WHY **ME**?
YOU'RE GOING TO DO GREAT THINGS IN CANADA, NIMO. WE BELIEVE IN YOU.
IT'S OK. DON'T WORRY ABOUT US. WE'LL BE FINE.
EVERYTHING WILL BE OK.

APOLOGISING TO JERI WAS HARDER FOR SOME REASON.

JUST TALK TO HIM!

BUT EVERY TIME I TRIED...

...I CHICKENED OUT.

JERI WAS MY BEST FRIEND, AND YET I'D BEEN SO FOCUSED ON MYSELF THE PAST FEW WEEKS, I NEVER ONCE THOUGHT ABOUT HOW **HE** WAS FEELING. SHAME BURNED HOT IN MY CHEST.

THIS WASN'T THE FIRST TIME I'D BEEN SO SELFISH. WHY ON EARTH WOULD HE KEEP TAKING A FRIEND LIKE ME BACK?

THE NIGHT BEFORE NIMO AND HER FAMILY LEFT, THE ENTIRE BLOCK CAME BY HER FAMILY'S HOME TO SAY GOODBYE.

I ALWAYS IMAGINED IF I LEFT DADAAB, I WOULD BE LAUGHING AND FEELING LIKE THE HAPPIEST PERSON IN THE WORLD...

...BUT EVERYONE IN NIMO'S FAMILY WAS CRYING.

FOR THE FIRST TIME, IT TRULY DAWNED ON ME HOW **SCARY** THIS MUST BE FOR NIMO. DADAAB MAY BE A REFUGEE CAMP, BUT IT'S THE ONLY HOME WE'VE EVER REALLY KNOWN.

HOOYO! HOOYO!

HOOYO!

STOP! COME BACK!

HASSAN!

HEY, HASSAN! HASSAN! CALM DOWN, BUDDY, IT'S OK!

HE'S HAPPY TO SEE YOU.

YEAH, SOMEHOW I GOT THAT.

JERI, I'M...

I KNOW.

I HAD BEEN A HORRIBLE FRIEND TO JERI. NO ONE WOULD WANT A FRIEND LIKE ME BACK.

BUT THE GOOD NEWS WAS, WE WEREN'T FRIENDS.
WE WERE BROTHERS.
AND THE THING ABOUT A BROTHER IS, YOU DON'T NEED WORDS TO UNDERSTAND EACH OTHER.

PART 3

FOUR YEARS LATER

THIS IS ME NOW. I LOOK PRETTY MUCH THE SAME AT SEVENTEEN AS I DID WHEN I WAS THIRTEEN. I'M NOT EVEN THAT MUCH TALLER, UNFORTUNATELY.

JERI IS TALLER. **MUCH** TALLER.

JERI AND I BOTH PASSED OUR KCPE* EXAMS, SO WE'RE AMONG THE FEW STUDENTS IN A2 FROM OUR GRADE TO GO TO SECONDARY SCHOOL. I'M REALLY PROUD OF THAT.

THE WHOLE NEIGHBOURHOOD IS PROUD OF US FOR GOING TO SECONDARY SCHOOL.

WE'RE KIND OF LIKE LOCAL CELEBRITIES!

*KCPE= KENYA CERTIFICIATE OF PRIMARY EDUCATION. THESE ARE THE LONG AND DIFFICULT EXAMS YOU HAVE TO PASS IN ORDER TO ATTEND SECONDARY SCHOOL.

FATUMA? HASSAN?

FATUMA IS ASLEEP. THAT MEANS HASSAN MUST BE WITH MARYAM.

I START A FIRE TO HEAT UP DINNER.

I CHANGE OUT OF MY UNIFORM. I WASH IT EVERY NIGHT TO KEEP IT LOOKING NICE AND CRISP.

EVEN THOUGH I PASSED MY EXAMS, I ALMOST DIDN'T GET TO GO TO SECONDARY SCHOOL BECAUSE I COULDN'T AFFORD A UNIFORM. LUCKILY, SUSANA MARTINEZ—THE SPANISH UN WORKER WHO VISITED MY MIDDLE SCHOOL? SHE CAME LOOKING FOR ME WHEN SHE HEARD I PASSED MY KCPE EXAMS. I THINK MICHAEL TOLD HER. WHEN SHE LEARNED I COULDN'T BUY A UNIFORM, SHE BOUGHT ONE FOR ME.

I COULDN'T BELIEVE SHE REMEMBERED ME AND WANTED TO HELP.

SOMETIMES I THINK FATUMA IS RIGHT—YOU JUST TRY YOUR BEST, AND GOD WILL FIND A WAY TO HELP YOU WHEN YOU NEED IT.

HOOYO!

HASSAN IS ALSO...

AAAAAAAAGH!

...BIGGER.

MARYAM IS BIGGER TOO. AGAIN.

HASSAN STILL SPENDS TIME WITH MARYAM NEARLY EVERY AFTERNOON. SHE'S ESPECIALLY GRATEFUL FOR HIS HELP THESE DAYS. HASSAN IS VERY ATTENTIVE TO LITTLE NIMO, AND HE LOVES PLAYING WITH HER.

LITTLE NIMO TAKES AFTER HER NAMESAKE.

HI OMAR!!! GUESS WHAT WE DID TODAY? WE PLAYED ON THE SWING! GUESS WHAT ELSE? I CAN WRITE MY NAME! AND GUESS WHAT ELSE? I CAN COUNT TO TEN!

NIMO IS TOO YOUNG FOR SCHOOL...BUT MARYAM IS ALREADY STARTING HER EDUCATION. MARYAM STILL STUDIES WHENEVER SHE CAN. SHE EVEN HELPS SOME OF THE NEIGHBOURHOOD GIRLS WITH THEIR HOMEWORK.
I GUESS THERE IS MORE THAN ONE WAY TO BECOME A TEACHER.
SOUNDS LIKE YOU'RE VERY SMART, JUST LIKE YOUR MAMA!
MAYBE SHE'LL EARN THAT SCHOLARSHIP TO CANADA SOMEDAY.
MARYAM LOOKS PROUD... BUT SAD TOO.
DID YOU HEAR THAT NIMO'S FAMILY CALLED FROM CANADA THE OTHER DAY? ALI FROM THE MARKET TOLD ME HER MOTHER WAS ON THE PHONE, AND I WAS ABLE TO SPEAK WITH NIMO FOR A FEW MINUTES.
NIMO SAYS IT'S REALLY HARD SPEAKING ENGLISH ALL THE TIME. THERE ARE ONLY A FEW OTHER SOMALI FAMILIES IN HER TOWN.
SHE ALSO SAID THAT NOT EVERYONE IN CANADA IS RICH—THAT LIFE IS NOT AS EASY AS SHE THOUGHT. SOME PEOPLE THERE LIVE OUT ON THE STREET.
SHE EVEN SAID SHE MISSES THE **FOOD** HERE IN DADAAB. CAN YOU BELIEVE THAT?
...NO.

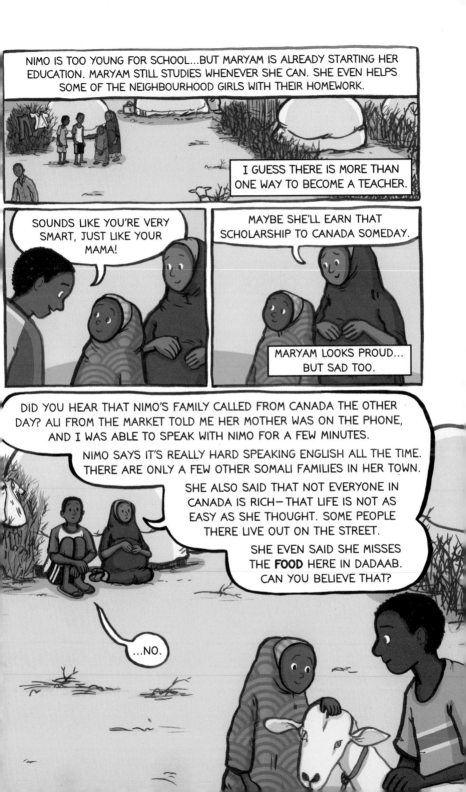

IT'S HARD TO IMAGINE THAT **ANYONE** WOULD MISS LIVING IN A REFUGEE CAMP.

AND YET, IT'S THE PLACE I CALL HOME.

SOON IT'S TIME FOR SUPPER, AND MARYAM AND NIMO HEAD BACK.

BYE-BYE, OMAR! BYE-BYE, HASSAN! I LOVE YOU!

I HEAT UP OUR SUPPER, AND I WAKE FATUMA WHEN IT'S READY.

FATUMA IS THE ONE PERSON WHO IS NOT GETTING BIGGER. IN FACT, SHE SEEMS TO BE SHRINKING.

BEFORE SHE EVEN THINKS OF EATING ANYTHING HERSELF, SHE MAKES SURE THE GOATS HAVE WATER.

THE GOATS ARE SHRINKING TOO. THERE ISN'T MUCH GRASS FOR THEM TO EAT THESE DAYS. NOW THAT THE CAMP IS GETTING BIGGER AND MORE CROWDED, RESOURCES LIKE FIREWOOD AND GRASS ARE HARDER TO FIND. FATUMA FRETS AND WORRIES OVER THEM ALL THE TIME.

JERI COMES OVER TO STUDY ALMOST EVERY NIGHT AFTER HE CHECKS ON HIS MUM AND SIBLINGS. BUT HIS DAD IS HARDLY EVER AROUND ANYMORE, SO THAT'S **ONE** THING HE DOESN'T HAVE TO WORRY ABOUT.

WE HAVE LOTS OF HOMEWORK IN SECONDARY SCHOOL. JERI SHARES HIS LAMP, AND I SHARE THE PEACE AND QUIET OF MY TENT.

...OF COURSE, "PEACE AND QUIET" IS STILL A RELATIVE TERM.

HASSAN! BUDDY! WE HAVE A BIG PAPER DUE TOMORROW, SO KEEP IT DOWN, ALL RIGHT?

THIS PAPER IS FOR ENGLISH CLASS. I FEEL LIKE I'VE HAD TO WRITE THIS SAME PAPER ABOUT TWENTY DIFFERENT TIMES IN ALL THE YEARS I'VE BEEN IN SCHOOL.

What It Means to Be a Refugee

JEEZ, CAN'T OUR TEACHERS BE A LITTLE MORE CREATIVE?!

Being a refugee means you don't have a home. I am Somali, but I can't go back to Somalia. I can't stay here in Kenya. I am stuck in the middle.

Being a refugee means...

BEING A REFUGEE MEANS I AM ALWAYS WORRIED ABOUT MY BROTHER. HE NEEDS MEDICAL TREATMENT, BUT THE DOCTORS HERE CAN'T STOP HIS SEIZURES. HE HASN'T HAD ONE IN A WHILE...BUT WHO KNOWS WHEN THE NEXT ONE WILL HAPPEN?

BEING A REFUGEE MEANS I AM WORRIED ABOUT FATUMA. I NEVER THOUGHT ABOUT IT AS A KID...BUT WHY IS SHE ALWAYS SO QUIET? SHE LOOKS WORRIED AND ANXIOUS ALL THE TIME, LIKE SHE IS ALWAYS THINKING ABOUT SOMETHING THAT UPSETS HER.

BEING A REFUGEE MEANS I AM WORRIED ABOUT MY FUTURE. IF I CAN'T WORK, HOW CAN I SUPPORT MY FAMILY? FATUMA IS GETTING WEAKER. HOW CAN I CARE FOR HER, AND MY BROTHER, AND STILL EARN MONEY?

BEING A REFUGEE MEANS YOU DON'T REALLY HAVE A FUTURE.

I hope that peace comes to Somalia so I can go back to my country and support my family.

OH YEAH— PEACE AND LOVE. TEACHERS ALWAYS LIKE WHEN YOU WRITE ABOUT PEACE AND LOVE.

EVERY DAY THAT PASSED BROUGHT ME A LITTLE CLOSER TO MY SECONDARY SCHOOL GRADUATION...AND THAT SCARED ME. I **LIKED** LEARNING—I DIDN'T WANT TO STOP.

AND DESPITE ALL THOSE ESSAYS WE WROTE ABOUT WHAT WE WANTED TO BE WHEN WE GREW UP...I STILL DIDN'T KNOW IF I COULD FIND A **JOB**.

AND IF I COULDN'T FIND A JOB...WHAT WOULD I DO TO FILL MY TIME?

I STARTED SEEING SOME OF OUR FORMER CLASSMATES HANGING AROUND THE KHAT STAND IN THE MARKET. CLASSMATES LIKE TALL ALI.

I'M ASHAMED TO ADMIT IT, BUT I UNDERSTOOD THE APPEAL OF KHAT SOMETIMES. WHEN PEOPLE ARE SUFFERING—AND YOU CAN'T DO ANYTHING TO HELP...YOU WANT TO FORGET.

SOMETIMES I FEEL SO HOPELESS IN THIS PLACE, I DON'T THINK I CAN STAND IT.

I'M SO THANKFUL FOR JERI. AT LEAST WE ARE HERE TOGETHER. WE'LL ALWAYS HAVE EACH OTHER'S BACK.

NOOOOOOOO!!!

FATUMA! WHAT'S WRONG?

HE WAS HUNGRY, AND I DIDN'T HAVE ANY FOOD TO GIVE HIM!

IN ALL THESE YEARS LIVING IN A REFUGEE CAMP, I'D NEVER SEEN FATUMA CRY ABOUT ANYTHING. AND HERE SHE WAS CRYING...ABOUT A GOAT.

IF I'D BEEN A BETTER MOTHER... IF I'D TAKEN BETTER CARE OF HIM...

HE WAS INNOCENT AND SWEET. HE DIDN'T DESERVE TO DIE.

SHE SAT THERE, CRADLING HER BABY GOAT FOR A LONG TIME. IT LOOKED LIKE THE WAY SHE USED TO HOLD ME AND HASSAN.

THE CRYING, THE DEAD BABY GOAT...SO MUCH SADNESS...

...IT WAS ALL TOO MUCH FOR HASSAN.

HASSAN! STOP! COME BACK!

YOU GO AFTER HASSAN. I'LL TAKE CARE OF EVERYTHING HERE.

IT'S BEEN A LONG TIME SINCE HASSAN HAS RUN OFF LIKE THIS. WHEN HE WAS LITTLE, IT WASN'T SO HARD TO FIND HIM. BUT HE'S BIGGER AND FASTER NOW.

HASSAN!

EXCUSE ME. SORRY.

HASSAN!

I SEARCHED FOR HOURS. WORD STARTED TO SPREAD THAT HASSAN WAS MISSING. ALL OF OUR NEIGHBOURS CAME OUT TO HELP.

HE—HE LIKES TO FEED THE DONKEYS IN THE MARKET. OR MAYBE THE BUILDING PIT? OR MAYBE...

NO. IT'S TOO DARK OUT IN THE BUSH. TOO DANGEROUS. HE COULD MEET ALL SORTS OF DANGEROUS ANIMALS...OR PEOPLE...OUT THERE ALL ALONE.

OMAR, IT'S GETTING TOO DARK. WE'LL HAVE TO WAIT UNTIL MORNING TO CONTINUE THE SEARCH.

EVER SINCE I GOT TO THIS REFUGEE CAMP, PEOPLE HAVE BEEN TELLING ME TO WAIT. WAIT FOR THE WAR TO BE OVER, WAIT TO BE RESETTLED, WAIT FOR NEWS OF YOUR MOTHER...

TONIGHT, I'M DONE WAITING.

I'M GOING TO FIND MY BROTHER.
I WALKED AND WALKED AND WALKED.
AS MORNING BROKE, I REACHED THE NEXT CAMP OVER—**DAGAHALEY** CAMP.
I ASKED EVERYONE I MET IF THEY HAD SEEN MY BROTHER.
NO LUCK.

DAGAHALEY WAS A LOT LIKE IFO CAMP. BIG FAMILIES LIVING IN SMALL TENTS. LONG LINES FOR WATER. THE SAME LOUDSPEAKER THAT, FIVE TIMES A DAY, CALLED EVERYONE TO PRAYER. JUST LIKE US.
I STARTED TO FEEL HOPELESS IN THIS ENDLESS SEA OF REFUGEES.
THERE WERE SO MANY OF US. THOUSANDS OF US. **HUNDREDS** OF THOUSANDS.
WHAT HOPE WAS THERE FOR US—FOR **ANY** OF US—TO FIND WHAT WE WERE SEARCHING FOR?
ATTENTION. TO THE YOUNG MAN LOOKING FOR YOUR BROTHER.

YOUR BROTHER IS HERE, HE IS SAFE. COME TO THE FRUIT STAND IN THE MARKET.
AGAIN, TO THE YOUNG MAN SEARCHING FOR YOUR BROTHER. HE IS SAFE. HE IS HERE.
MY...I'M LOOKING FOR... IS HE HERE?
AH! SO YOU ARE THE YOUNG MAN LOOKING FOR YOUR BROTHER. COME WITH ME! HE IS SAFE AT MY HOME.
I MET YOUR BROTHER LATE LAST NIGHT—HE WAS WANDERING AROUND THE MARKET. HE COULDN'T TELL ME HIS NAME OR WHERE HE WAS FROM, BUT I FIGURED SOMEONE WOULD COME LOOKING FOR HIM. THEN THIS MORNING, MY NEIGHBOUR TELLS ME A YOUNG MAN WAS LOOKING FOR HIS BROTHER—I GUESS THAT'S YOU!
MY WIFE IS CARING FOR HIM NOW...

MUNIRA! WE HAVE A VISITOR!

I THOUGHT I'D LOST YOU.

BUT I DIDN'T LOSE HIM. WE STILL HAD EACH OTHER.

PLEASE, HAVE SOME TEA WITH US.

SOMETIMES, WHEN LIFE FEELS LIKE IT'S AT ITS LOWEST...

THIS IS OUR DAUGHTER, SARURA.

...GOD WILL DELIVER AN ANSWER, AND YOU'LL FIND A PATH OUT OF THE DARKNESS.

THE KINDNESS OF STRANGERS. THE PROMISE OF NEW FRIENDS.

LIFE IS ALWAYS THE SAME IN A REFUGEE CAMP...

...EXCEPT WHEN IT'S **NOT**.

SOMETIMES YOUR LIFE CAN CHANGE IN AN INSTANT, BUT YOU CAN NEVER BE SURE IF IT'S A **GOOD** CHANGE OR A **BAD** CHANGE.

HELLO, SALAN.

HI, JERI. HI, MARYAM.

<SUSANA? WHY ARE **YOU** HERE?>

I DON'T UNDERSTAND, FATUMA. IS EVERYONE HERE BECAUSE HASSAN IS BACK?

NO, OMAR. EVERYONE IS HERE BECAUSE YOU WILL BE **LEAVING**. YOUR NAMES ARE ON THE LIST WITH THE UN. YOU'RE GOING BACK FOR A SECOND INTERVIEW...TO BE RESETTLED TO AMERICA.

CHAPTER 15

I DIDN'T BELIEVE IT WAS REAL...NOT FOR A LONG TIME. I HAD WASTED MONTHS—**YEARS**—OF MY LIFE, WAITING AND HOPING TO BE RESETTLED TO ANOTHER COUNTRY.

BUT EVEN IN A REFUGEE CAMP, MY FATE IS IN MY HANDS. I WASN'T GOING TO WASTE ANOTHER MINUTE OF MY LIFE HOPING FOR THE IMPOSSIBLE.

SO I KEEP GOING TO SCHOOL, EVERY DAY.

I KEEP FETCHING WATER.

I KEEP CARING FOR MY FAMILY AS BEST I CAN.

UNTIL IT IS THE DAY BEFORE OUR INTERVIEW.

DO YOU WANT TO REHEARSE YOUR STORY AGAIN?

NO. IF I DON'T KNOW MY LIFE STORY BY NOW, I'LL NEVER KNOW IT.

WELL– WE SHOULD PROBABLY LEAVE SOON. I THOUGHT WE'D CAMP OUT OVERNIGHT AGAIN. IT'S EVEN HARDER FOR YOU TO WALK NOW, SO IF WE LEAVE IN THE NEXT HOUR OR TWO, THAT WILL LEAVE US PLENTY OF TIME TO TAKE BREAKS ON THE WAY...
OMAR, I'M AN OLD WOMAN NOW. I CAN'T MAKE THAT LONG WALK AGAIN.
WHAT? WELL...I WISH YOU'D TOLD ME SOONER. MAYBE I CAN ASK ALI AT THE MARKET IF WE CAN BORROW HIS CART AND DONKEY...
NO. I'M AFRAID YOU'LL HAVE TO DO THIS ALONE. BESIDES, YOU'RE NEARLY EIGHTEEN NOW! YOU'RE NOT A CHILD ANY MORE, SO YOU DON'T NEED YOUR GUARDIAN WITH YOU.
WELL, YES...BUT YOU'RE OUR **GUARDIAN**. THE UN WILL NEED TO INTERVIEW YOU TOO.
TO COME WITH US.
TO COME TO AMERICA.

OMAR. LIKE I SAID, YOU'RE NOT A CHILD ANY MORE.

BUT...YOU WERE WITH US THE LAST TIME DURING THE INTERVIEWS!

DID THEY ASK ME ANY QUESTIONS? ASK ME ABOUT MY STORY? NO. SINCE I AM NOT **RELATED** TO YOU, I CAN'T COME WITH YOU TO AMERICA.

THIS IS ABOUT YOU AND HASSAN, OMAR. IT'S **ALWAYS** BEEN ABOUT YOU AND HASSAN.

BUT...

AND EVEN THOUGH I WAS ALMOST EIGHTEEN, I SAT DOWN AND CRIED LIKE THE LITTLE BOY I USED TO BE.

I FELT SO NAIVE FOR NOT SEEING THE TRUTH THAT WAS RIGHT BEFORE ME.

THEN I WON'T GO.

I WON'T LEAVE YOU, FATUMA!

243

OMAR, THE UNITED NATIONS MAY CALL ME YOUR GUARDIAN...BUT I **FEEL** LIKE YOUR MOTHER. AND A MOTHER WANTS HER CHILDREN TO MOVE ON. TO LEAD A BETTER LIFE THAN HERSELF. THAT'S WHAT A MOTHER'S LOVE DOES.

SO YES, OMAR. IF YOU LOVE ME... YOU WILL LEAVE ME. YOU MUST.

EVERYTHING WILL BE OK.

SO MY BROTHER AND I WENT ALONE.

WE WERE BACK IN THE UN OFFICES. WE HAD A DIFFERENT INTERVIEWER, BUT MAYBE THEY WERE RELATED, BECAUSE THEY SEEMED TO SHARE THE SAME INABILITY TO SMILE...

...DESPITE HASSAN'S BEST EFFORTS.

BY NOW I SPOKE ENGLISH WELL ENOUGH THAT I DIDN'T NEED AN INTERPRETER. I COULD SPEAK FOR MYSELF.

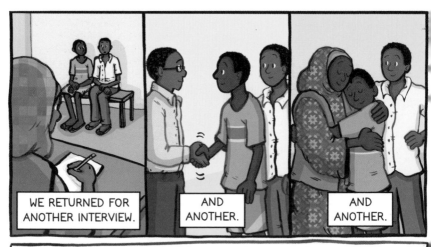

WE RETURNED FOR ANOTHER INTERVIEW.

AND ANOTHER.

AND ANOTHER.

I HAD PILES OF FORMS TO FILL OUT. SUSANA MARTINEZ HELPED ME WITH THE PAPERWORK SO I WOULDN'T MAKE ANY MISTAKES. ANY SMALL MISTAKE, AND YOUR APPLICATION COULD BE DENIED.

THE PROCESS WAS LONG AND GRUELLING, BUT I WASN'T AS NERVOUS. I WAS CALM.

THE UNITED NATIONS MAY DECIDE WHETHER I LEAVE OR I STAY... BUT ONLY I COULD DECIDE WHAT I WOULD MAKE OF MY LIFE.

SO DURING THE MONTHS OF WAITING TO HEAR BACK FROM THE UN, I KEPT GOING TO SCHOOL AND WORKING HARD.

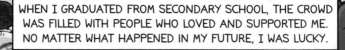

WHEN I GRADUATED FROM SECONDARY SCHOOL, THE CROWD WAS FILLED WITH PEOPLE WHO LOVED AND SUPPORTED ME. NO MATTER WHAT HAPPENED IN MY FUTURE, I WAS LUCKY.

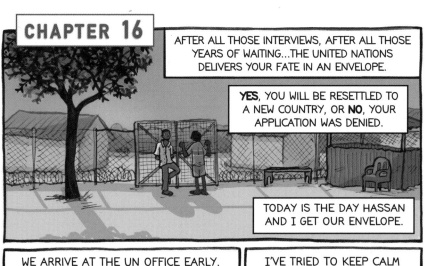

CHAPTER 16

AFTER ALL THOSE INTERVIEWS, AFTER ALL THOSE YEARS OF WAITING...THE UNITED NATIONS DELIVERS YOUR FATE IN AN ENVELOPE.

YES, YOU WILL BE RESETTLED TO A NEW COUNTRY, OR **NO**, YOUR APPLICATION WAS DENIED.

TODAY IS THE DAY HASSAN AND I GET OUR ENVELOPE.

WE ARRIVE AT THE UN OFFICE EARLY. SUSANA IS WAITING OUTSIDE TO GREET US.

<ARE YOU NERVOUS?>

I'VE TRIED TO KEEP CALM ABOUT OUR CHANCES, BUT TODAY...

<YES. I'M REALLY, REALLY NERVOUS.>

HOOYO! HOOYO!

<DO YOU KNOW, AFTER ALL THESE YEARS, THAT'S THE ONLY SOUND I'VE EVER HEARD HASSAN SAY? I WONDER WHAT IT MEANS...>

I'M SO SURPRISED, I FORGET MY NERVOUSNESS FOR A MOMENT.

<BUT...I THOUGHT YOU KNEW. "HOOYO" ISN'T A SOUND—IT'S A **WORD**. A SOMALI WORD. IT'S THE ONLY WORD HASSAN HAS EVER SAID.>

HOOYO!

<"HOOYO" MEANS MAMA.>

<BUT...I DON'T UNDERSTAND. AFTER ALL THESE YEARS... YOUR MOTHER...>

<AFTER ALL THESE YEARS... MAYBE HE STILL HOPES WE CAN FIND HER.>

BUT I DON'T KNOW IF THIS IS TRUE.

MAYBE **I** AM THE ONE WHO STILL HOPES WE CAN FIND HER.

IF WE GO TO AMERICA, IF WE LEAVE AFRICA...WHAT HAPPENS TO THAT HOPE?

<THE OFFICE IS OPEN. IT'S TIME FOR YOU TO GO IN.

GOOD LUCK, YOU TWO.>

BUT WE DON'T NEED LUCK—WE'VE DONE ALL WE CAN. IT'S IN GOD'S HANDS NOW.

EVERYONE SAYS IT'S GOOD TO GET A **THICK** ENVELOPE. A THICK ENVELOPE MEANS YOU HAVE MORE PAPERWORK AND FORMS TO FILL OUT. A THIN ENVELOPE JUST MEANS NO.

THERE WERE LOTS OF OTHER FAMILIES WAITING WITH US. ONE BY ONE, THEIR NAMES WERE CALLED. SOME FAMILIES GOT THIN ENVELOPES. SOME GOT THICK ONES. EITHER WAY, MOST OF THE PEOPLE WAITING WERE CRYING.

MOHAMED, OMAR. MOHAMED, HASSAN.

THAT'S US.

WE STOOD UP. HASSAN AND I WALKED TO THE UN OFFICER, ONE FOOT IN FRONT OF THE OTHER.

CHAPTER 17

THE NEXT MONTHS WERE A BLUR OF SECURITY SCREENINGS,

MEDICAL EXAMINATIONS,

AND IDENTIFICATION DOCUMENTS.

FLASH

AT ANY POINT, OUR CASE COULD HAVE BEEN DENIED. BUT WE WERE LUCKY.

AFTER YEARS OF WAITING, EVERYTHING WAS MOVING SO FAST. ONLY A FEW MONTHS LATER, IT'S TIME TO SAY GOODBYE.

TALL SALAN.

I HAVE A PRESENT FOR YOU.

IT'S A BOTTLE FILLED WITH SAND FROM DADAAB. MAY YOUR BLESSINGS BE AS COUNTLESS AS THE GRAINS OF SAND IN THE DESERT AND THE STARS IN THE SKY.

I AM SAYING GOODBYE TO MY HOME.

THIS IS FOR YOU.

MY FAMILY.

HOOYO!

IT'S OK.

EVERYTHING WILL BE OK.

I'M SAYING GOODBYE TO THE GHOST OF MY FATHER.

THE HOPE OF MY MOTHER.

HOOYO.

I THINK ABOUT THAT WORD. THE ONLY WORD HASSAN HAS EVER SAID. I CAN'T REMEMBER THE LAST TIME **I** SAID IT.

HOOYO.
MAMA.

IN A REFUGEE CAMP, YOU ARE ALWAYS REMINDED OF THE THINGS YOU HAVE LOST. IT IS A VALIANT AND AGONISING STRUGGLE TO FOCUS NOT ON WHAT YOU HAVE **LOST**...BUT ON WHAT YOU HAVE BEEN **GIVEN**.

MANY YEARS AGO, WE LOST OUR MOTHER.

BUT MAYBE SHE IS NOT GONE.

SHE IS IN THE LOVE THAT SURROUNDS US AND THE PEOPLE WHO CARE FOR US.

MAYBE SHE IS IN THE VERY SAND BENEATH OUR FEET.

SO PERHAPS WE'RE NOT LEAVING OUR MOTHER BEHIND. MAYBE SHE'LL ALWAYS BE WITH US. EVEN IN AMERICA.

I CAN ONLY THINK OF ONE THING TO SAY TO HASSAN, AS WE LEAVE OUR HOME.

HOOYO.

A Poem of Stars
by Maryam Farah

Those who are lost
look to the stars to lead
them home.

JOMO KENYA
TERMIN
Dep
Arri
In

The flag of Somalia, our home, has one
star, one background.

But we are not one star. We are
millions. Not one background,
but millions.

255

To the untrained eye, the night sky is a scattering of stars, a chaos of light and dark across the universe.
C1-C22
And yet, the stars are not lost.
C12
They form patterns. Constellations. If you know how to look, there are stories woven into the very essence of stars.
Be like a star. Shine your light. Shine your story.
For stories will lead us home.

FOR ME, THE FIRST YEARS ARE LOST.
I HOPE THAT IN AMERICA, HASSAN AND I WILL FIND OUR WAY.

2008, BEFORE LEAVING DADAAB.
FATUMA, HASSAN, OMAR

2008, BEFORE LEAVING DADAAB.
HASSAN, OMAR

GRADUATION,
UNIVERSITY OF ARIZONA

OMAR ON A RECENT TRIP BACK TO DADAAB.
OMAR, HASSAN, THEIR MOTHER, AND
TWO OF OMAR'S CHILDREN

DISTRIBUTING SUPPLIES TO STUDENTS IN DADAAB WITH REFUGEE STRONG

AFTERWORD

Omar and Hassan left Dadaab and arrived in the United States in January 2009. They were resettled in Tucson, Arizona, where they lived in a one-bedroom apartment together. The streets in Tucson were quiet and empty, and it was unsettling not seeing anybody walking around outside. After four months, Omar got his first job; he was a pool attendant at a fancy resort. The pool had water slides and a floating basketball net, and guests to the hotel included Tiger Woods and President Bush. Such luxury was so strange to see after living in Dadaab.

Doctors in the US were able to give Hassan medication to better control his seizures and to help him sleep at night. He began attending classes at an adult care centre in Tucson. Omar, too, continued his education; after a year, Omar went to college at the University of Arizona. He majored in International Development, with an emphasis on development in Africa. He graduated in 2014, the same year he and Hassan became citizens of the United States.

During this time, Omar had kept in touch with an old friend from Dadaab: Sarura. Her family had taken care of Hassan when he ran away to Dagahaley camp. Sarura's family had also been resettled to the United States, in Pennsylvania. Sarura moved to Arizona, and she and Omar were married and began a family. In 2015, Omar accepted a position as a resettlement case manager at Church World Service in Lancaster, Pennsylvania, to be closer to Sarura's family. Omar was finally a social worker, just as he'd always dreamed. Hassan lives with Omar and Sarura in Pennsylvania and helps care for their five young children.

Throughout this time, Omar had not given up on what seemed to be an impossible dream: to find their mother. When civil war broke out in Somalia in 1991, it was not unusual for families to become separated. Children and grown-ups alike were forced to drop everything and run, whether they were at work, school, or the market. It could take months or years for families to reunite, often through word-of-mouth. Through his work as a resettlement case manager, Omar met many new arrivals from Dadaab and other refugee camps in Kenya. He asked every new arrival if they had any information on a woman from Mareerey who had lost her husband and two boys.

In 2014, a woman named Hawa Ali arrived in Ifo camp. She was looking for her two sons. She had been told years ago that the boys had passed away, but she had never stopped searching. Neighbours directed her to Fatuma's tent. Fatuma showed Hawa a photograph of Omar and Hassan. Hawa was able to see her sons for the first time in twenty-three years.

In 2017, Omar and Hassan were able to make the journey back to Kenya to reunite with their mother. Hawa still lives in Dadaab and various refugee camps around Kenya. Omar is working to secure papers to allow her to join her sons in the United States. The current (2019) travel restrictions against people born in Somalia means that their mother can't join them now. But this family is used to waiting, and they are hopeful for the future.

The United Nations estimates that in 2019, there are nearly 71 million people who have been forcibly displaced from their homes worldwide. Most of the people displaced from their homes come from developing countries. You can visit www.unhcr.org to learn more about the worldwide refugee crisis. Many towns and cities in the United States have nonprofits and organisations to help new arrivals to the US settle into their new homes. You can often donate clothing, school supplies and home goods to refugee families right in your own community.

Omar is the founder of a project called Refugee Strong. He organises volunteer trips to Dadaab once or twice a year. With the funds he raises throughout the year, he delivers books, pencils and lamps to students. Refugee Strong also focuses on helping girls continue their studies by delivering menstrual hygiene products and building toilets for girls – two major stumbling blocks that keep girls from attending classes.

If you would like to get involved, please visit
WWW.REFUGEESTRONG.ORG to learn more.

AUTHOR'S NOTE
OMAR MOHAMED

Born in Somalia, I fled with my brother, Hassan, to Dadaab Refugee Camp in Kenya at age four, and then spent the next fifteen years there. Dadaab is referred to as an "Open Prison" by the refugees living there because they are not allowed to leave the camp. Despite the difficulties of life at the camp, I completed primary and secondary school in Dadaab.

I cannot talk about my time in the camp without mentioning the one person who had the most influence on my life. Her name is Susana Martinez, and she worked with UNHCR in the Community Service Programme. Susana never stopped watching over my brother and me; she would always look for us when she visited the camp. Hassan and I were very disappointed when we heard the news that Susana had been transferred to Bangladesh. When she got to Bangladesh, Susana asked the resettlement agency in Dadaab to follow up with us, and that was when they finally reached out. I fully believe that she shaped me into the person I am today. Without her, I may not have been resettled or have even completed secondary. I thank Susana for her kindness, and I will always continue to help others and provide support like Susana did for me and Hassan.

My wife, Sarura, and I still live near Lancaster, Pennsylvania, with our five children, in a community that is home to many other resettled refugees from Dadaab. Hassan also lives with us and helps take care of the children. He still attends adult education classes, and the medical care he receives in the United States helps control his seizures and helps him sleep better at night. We are regularly in touch with our mother and Fatuma, and other friends and loved ones who still live in Dadaab, and visit whenever we can.

I have always wanted to write a book to educate others about my experience as a refugee. I had already started drafting my story when I met Victoria. The minute I first met with Vicki, I had confidence in sharing my story with her. I am impressed by her commitment and determination to work with me despite my busy daily life, which necessitates contacting me during my work lunch breaks, coming to my home late in the evening or early mornings, and using texts, calls, Facebook, and other creative communication techniques.

In my current role with Church World Service, I work with refugees from the first day they arrive in the US, helping them to reach self-sufficiency within the guidelines of the State Department. I am always motivated and encouraged by the success of those whom I have helped to resettle.

I am also the founder of a project called Refugee Strong, which focuses on improving and making education available to all children in refugee camps. Twice in the last few years, I have returned to Dadaab to volunteer in the schools as a mentor. With the help of CWS-Lancaster and the greater Lancaster community, Refugee Strong was able to deliver school supplies to the students who are unable to afford them. Having grown up in Dadaab, I am a constant advocate for those who continue living in any refugee camp around the world.

Empowering and supporting refugees is key to helping them succeed not only in the camps but also in their new communities. No one chooses to be a refugee, to leave their home, country and family. The last thing I wanted in this world was to be a refugee. I have worked hard to overcome my challenges as a refugee, but I would not have been able to do it without the staff of UNHCR, Save the Children, World Food Programme, Care International, Church World Service, the Islamic Community Center of Lancaster, PACRI and the DSAK Foundation. I would also like to thank Dawna Foster, my mentor at the University of Arizona. I am grateful to the Garver family, who became very close with me and my family. Thank you to all of the individuals and organisations who have helped and supported me along the way.

I want to thank my wife, Sarura, for all her support. She is a very patient and caring mother and wife. The way she loves and cares for Hassan has created a remarkable bond between the two of them, and this is an additional blessing to me.

Please take away from the reading of this book an understanding that you should never give up hope. In the camp, we were given courage by our faith to always be patient and to never lose hope. Things may seem impossible, but if you keep working hard and believe in yourself, you can overcome anything in your path. I hope that my story will inspire you to always persevere.

AUTHOR'S NOTE
VICTORIA JAMIESON

The seeds for *When Stars Are Scattered* were first planted in my life in 2016. The world around me seemed to be growing increasingly chaotic, and the news was filled with stories of Syrian refugees fleeing their homes. I wanted to gain a better understanding of the issue, so I began volunteering with a nonprofit in my community, greeting arriving refugee families at the airport, and later working as a cultural liaison.

I began to wonder if there might be a way I could put my background as a graphic novelist to use. I love graphic novels because they are such an intimate reading experience. What would it be like to read a graphic novel about one person's life as a refugee? When I met Omar through his work at Church World Service, he was already working on a memoir geared toward adults and was looking for a coauthor. I told him that adult books were not my area of expertise, and asked if he had ever considered writing his story as a children's book. We sat down to talk about what that might look like; *When Stars Are Scattered* is the answer.

This is Omar's story, and I tried to change as little as possible as I adapted it into a graphic novel. My first priority, in every step of the process, was making sure I was being true to his memories and experiences. To write this book, Omar and I would meet every few weeks, and he would tell me another chapter of his life story. I would write it up, send it to him, and we'd meet again to discuss the details. Eventually, I began adding sketches and setting the story in a graphic novel format. When I had to invent characters, like Nimo and Maryam, I based them on Omar's memories and my own research. I am incredibly grateful to Omar for his bravery and willingness to share his story with young readers. I am humbled and honoured that he trusted me with this project. The greatest privilege of working on this book has been getting to know Omar and his family, as well as our colourist, Iman Geddy. As a graphic novelist, I am used to telling stories; working on this book with Omar and Iman has taught me it is equally important to listen to stories.

I am also grateful for you, young readers, for picking up this book and reading about the experiences of someone else. Maybe Omar's story is similar to your story, the story of someone in your family, someone in your town, or maybe he is like no one you've ever met before. I wanted to write this book for you because I know that young people have the most compassionate, open hearts, and that you have the energy to truly make a difference. I hope that you'll look at Omar's website and think of ways your school or community can participate in empowering the thousands of kids who still live and go to school in refugee camps, or new refugee families right in your own town. Lastly, I hope that you will be inspired to talk with someone new. Maybe there's a new kid at your school or a new family in your neighbourhood. Maybe there's a kid you've seen for years but have never spoken to. Try it. Talk to them. Ask them their name, where they're from, what kind of food they like to eat, what TV shows they like to watch. You'll hear some amazing stories when you talk to someone new.

ACKNOWLEDGEMENTS

Many people contributed their time and energy to the creation of this book. To our many beta readers who gave feedback on early versions of this story, we thank you. Your knowledge, expertise and experiences helped shape this book, and we couldn't have done it without you.

To the staff of Church World Service in Lancaster, Pennsylvania, thank you for your support and enthusiasm for this project. Thank you to Emily Cintora for providing photographs from Dadaab.

Our publishing team at Dial Books for Young Readers worked tirelessly to make this book the very best it could be. Our editor, Kate Harrison, publisher Lauri Hornik, and art director Jason Henry were with us every step of the way. To everyone at Dial: Ellen Cormier, Nancy Mercado, Lily Malcolm, Regina Castillo, Rachel Wease, Carmela Iaria, Vanessa Carson, Trevor Ingerson, Summer Ogata, Elyse Marshall, Christina Colangelo, Emily Romero, and the rest of the gang – thank you for the amazing work you do. Thank you to Paul Rodeen, agent extraordinaire. Iman Geddy supplied the amazing colours (and amazing encouragement!) that saw this project across the finish line.

To our families, thank you for the support and love during the long process of making a graphic novel.

Lastly, thank you to all new immigrants to the US – for sharing their stories with us, and for making this country a richer place to live.

OMAR MOHAMED & VICTORIA JAMIESON